IT'S BEEN
ONE OF THOSE DAYS,
LORD

IT'S BEEN
ONE OF THOSE DAYS,
LORD

BOB W. BROWN

Daybreak Books

Zondervan Publishing House
Grand Rapids, Michigan

Daybreak Books are published by
Zondervan Publishing House
1415 Lake Drive, S.E.
Grand Rapids, MI 49506

IT'S BEEN ONE OF THOSE DAYS, LORD
Copyright © 1971 by Zondervan Publishing House
Revised edition copyright © 1985 by The Zondervan Corporation
Grand Rapids, Michigan

Library of Congress Cataloging in Publication Data

Brown, Bob W.
    It's been one of those days, Lord.   1 - 86

    1. Pastoral theology.   I. Title.
BV4014.B74   1985   253'.2   85-91272
ISBN 0-310-28912-2

Edited and designed by Julie Ackerman Link

Printed in the United States of America

85   86   87   88   89   90   /   15   14   13   12   11   10   9   8

To my mother and dad
who taught me to pray
during "those days"

CONTENTS

On Praying 13
Hardin 14
A Cemetery 15
A Family Fight 16
The Arnolds 17
Another Day 18
The Purple Plum 20
Jolly George 21
My Home Town 22
The Wedding 23
A Weight Watcher 24
Fishing 25
Patsy 26
Gene 27
A Boy and His Friends 28
First Day of School 30
Talk, Talk, Talk 31
Mr. Orville 32
A Quiet Time 33
Greed 34
Lucille 36
Ralph 37
At Night 38
Getting Attention 39
At 4:00 A.M 40
Brother Johnson 41
Speak, Lord 43
Things No One Wants 44
July 4th—Thanksgiving 45
My Teenager 46
Father's Day 47
A Commencement Speech 48
Patience 49
The Widower 50
Unity 51
The Old Man 52
The Expert 53
A Lone Daffodil 54

Just What We Need 55
The Unwed Father 56
Listening 57
Spiritual Things 59
Overflow 60
Why? 61
Daddy Won't Love Me Anymore 62
Too Late 63
The Cynic and the Snow 64
Sermons 65
Chester 67
The Bore 68
A Poor Drama 69
A New Father 70
Six Children 71
The Man Who Has Everything 72
Who Will See the Tree? 73
A Writer in the Ghetto 74
How High is Up? 75
The Ministerial Student 76
Self-righteous—Who Me? 77
Pat is Dead 79
The Second Time 80
The Hit-and-Run Driver 81
The Kids and Drugs 82
Right or Wrong 83
A Man 84
On War and Peace 86
I'm Tired 87
The Street Where I Live 88
Don't Be Afraid 89
For the New Parents 90
On Adopting a Child 91
He Never Wins 92
Man on the Moon 93
The Guy with Three Kids 94
Things Look Different 96
A Losing Battle 97
The Church 98
On Becoming Six 99

On Appearance Only 100
The High School Graduate 101
The Mother Without a Partner 102
The Childless Mother 103
A Man Named Chester 104
The College Boy 105
The Dog Killer 106
For a Boy Scout 107
The Boy Is Dead 108
The Old Folks 109
On a Hungry Child 110
For a Middle-aged Cop 111
Sweethearts 112
For Harlem 114
On a Blind Man 115
On Losing a Friend 116
A Broken Bird Egg 117
On Sunday Night 118
For a Poor Man 120
Birthday 121
The Little Wood Carver 122
About Losing 123
An Interruption 124
A Quiet Time 125
A Tribal God 126
A Good Night Kiss 127
Lonely 128
Melvin, the Black Child 129
For Billy Graham 131
The Golden Rule 132
Mr. President 133
A Little Boy 134
George 135
On Saying No 136
For Other Preachers 138
Talking Too Much 139
A Small Pleasure 140

PREFACE

In 1948 members of a little church called me to be their pastor. My concepts of the ministry were fuzzy. But I thought anyone could learn to be a successful pastor. I was eighteen and believed in education, training, and discipline. And I believed in God.

But my hang-ups were consistently about prayer. I tried to pray in appointed ways and at appropriate times. I read prayers ... wrote prayers ... said prayers. Sometimes I felt better. Sometimes worse. Sometimes my prayers were answered in detail. Sometimes my answer was silence.

Along the way I relaxed and began talking to God about things that bugged me. Usually other people, because my life is all tied up with other people. I'm not sure that much of this is really intercessory prayer. Or "powerful" prayer. But it is the way I pray.

Most people aren't interested in reading prayers. I'm not either. But the people in these prayers are interesting people. At least they kept my interest long enough for a prayer. You probably know people like them.

Thanks to the people in Trinity Church, to my own Helen, Jeff, and Amy. And to June Richey, my sister and reader. To my secretaries June Picklesimer, Lorraine Newton, and Lou Ann Sorrell.

And to our Lord Jesus who listens to all of my conversation on "Those Days."

Bob W. Brown
Lexington, Ky.

ON PRAYING

FATHER, I guess You know pretty well what I'm going to say before I say it. Most of us become predictable. It isn't hard to anticipate and expect particular reactions, conversation, and conduct from people we love. If we really love them, that is. And with all of my doubts, I don't doubt that You love me.

Funny about that. When I first started praying, it was some kind of formula deal with me. Get in the right posture. Find the right place. Say the right things. Say them the right way. And *shazam!* a miracle would happen. If the prayer wasn't answered right, then I assumed that somehow I had missed the formula for miracles.

Then I went through the impulsive, emotional praying stage. If I cried enough . . . or prayed hard enough . . . or confessed enough sin and orneriness, then You were bound to get busy.

After that it was the casual, conversational, sometimes cute and always clever prayer. Especially public prayers. And the nonconventional, clever phrases became conformist clichés. This was the kind of prayer people talked about. Fun to listen to and fun to do.

Often there was an exercise in futility. I've tried to pray when I didn't want to. When there wasn't anything to say. When I didn't really believe what I was saying. When I wondered where You were and sometimes even wondered "if" You are.

So, praying hasn't always been easy. Or even helpful. Or even right. But I know You love me. I know that.

No wonder the disciples said to You, "Lord, teach us to pray." Teach me, too.

HARDIN

FATHER, probably the hardest thing about preaching is trying to talk to a guy like Hardin. He is so self-confident. Capable. Secure. Arrogant and proud, I'm sure, but he isn't really offensive to me. The kind of man who acts as he does never needs advice, counsel, or help.

Hardin reads a lot and understands what he reads. He has intelligent opinions about a lot of things. He seems to exude success. His work prospers. He makes decisions quickly and sticks to them. He makes money with equal dispatch and enjoys it.

Hardin is a handsome, healthy fellow. A pretty wife and one son. She attends our church and so does the boy. But Hardin just doesn't need it. At least that's what he has always said. He doesn't think the church can make him healthy, wealthy, or wise. Always says that there isn't one good reason for him to attend church.

Well, now this boy of his, Allen, is in the hospital. All broken up in a car accident. Critical. In a coma. Breathing machines. Faint heart beat. Dying, I guess. He is in real bad shape, Lord.

So now Hardin needs me. He calls me. Wants me to be there. To pray. He wants me to produce a miracle out of some kind of religious top hat. Wave a wand. He is crying. Scared. Brokenhearted. Terrified.

Lord, he really loves that boy and wants him to live. He admits his sin. Says that he will serve You. He is begging.

As You know I have been pretty frustrated about Hardin over the past years. And I'm not sure about him, or about You, in this kind of sadness. But it sure would be something special if that boy could get well. Not that Hardin, or I, deserve anything extra from You. But if You would—You could. If not, I know You always have something good and right for us all.

A CEMETERY

FATHER, I was in the cemetery today. A fellow pointed out to me the Jewish section. I was in sight of a section for black people. And across the road was a Catholic cemetery. Of course they all had family plots, family sections.

Been thinking about that tonight. Not that it is the most important thing in the world, but it does say something about us. We are apparently determined, even in death, to keep our partitions and barriers up. And a graveyard with its special sections and special plots continues our separation.

I can't think of any logical reason for a Jewish, Gentile, Baptist, Catholic, black or white section of graveyard. But it is there.

Maybe there is as much reason for sections in a cemetery as there are reasons for sections in a city. Maybe there is as much logic to separating people in death as there is for separation in life.

Will we corrupt one another? Rub off? Ruin? Seems to me that this is contrary to the concept of Your creation. Surely You didn't make any of us better than anyone else. You made us all the same. You love us all the same.

And I know this business of separated sections in graveyards is contrary to the fact of death. There just isn't any difference in a graveyard. Everyone in them is the same.

They are dead.

Maybe we can learn something about living together if we see the ridiculousness of separated sections in graveyards.

A FAMILY FIGHT

FATHER, it doesn't happen often, but my wife and I had a verbal fight. The kids heard it. The neighbors might have heard it. You heard it. Now we're both sorry. And we'll make up. And we'll forget it. And the neighbors will forget. And You will forget. But it's not that easy for the kids.

I suppose children have always heard their parents quarrel. Marriage is a hard proposition at best. There are built-in tensions and pressures. Explosive situations. Difficult times. All of this makes us bark and bite, fume and fuss. So there is nothing unique about our spat.

But this is a miserable experience for children. They are frightened and dismayed when it happens. Their security is threatened. They don't understand.

They don't want to take sides and they have a terrible fear that the fight is permanent.

No child can comprehend the subtle and intimate nature of marital conflict. They don't know anything yet about anxiety, brooding love, or impotent failure. They don't realize that people have to be in love even to become angry.

So a fighting family tears a child up.

There is no way I can make my children understand why these things happen. And besides, I'm of no disposition or inclination to try to teach them.

The best alternative and most rational and loving answer is for us not to quarrel in front of the children. Surely You can help us suppress these periodic spats until we have some privacy.

I'm sorry about the fight. Sorry for the children. And I promise to make the next one a private affair.

THE ARNOLDS

FATHER, a doctor once told me that there were a hundred symptoms of every disease. The problem is isolating the symptoms, recognizing them, and diagnosing the disease on the basis of the symptoms. I guess the same thing is true in my work. But somehow my eyes don't see and my ears don't hear.

I'm upset tonight about the Arnolds. At one time they were both active in every church activity. Had a lot of friends. Three happy, well-adjusted children. I visited in their home. Conducted a funeral for her mother. They usually stopped by my house a couple of times a year to chat. We went to some ball games with them. I guess we were friends.

Then he started missing church services. Then he was working at another job. At least that's what they said. They said he didn't earn enough money at his former job.

Then she was in the hospital a couple of times. Stomach aches. Backaches. Headaches. Doctors ran tests. Couldn't find anything. She lost a lot of weight. She started dressing like her daughters.

He didn't have much to say to me. Changed jobs again. Chain smoking. He went to the hospital himself. Chronic headaches. Doctors told him to slow down, relax. He didn't go to ball games. Didn't seem to have friends anymore. The last time I saw him he was cross and irritable. Wanted to argue a lot about a local tax on phone calls.

The son joined the Marines. One of the girls wanted to get married at seventeen. The other girl is running wild. Missing school.

Today I read that the Arnolds are getting a divorce. I should have realized. Should have diagnosed. Perhaps I could have helped. But I missed on this one. Forgive me, Father.

ANOTHER DAY

FATHER, what a day. A couple of hours going over the church budget. There is never enough money to do all we need to do, but always enough to do some of the things we need to do. And I don't really enjoy raising, collecting, and spending money. But that's part of the job.

Thanks for the people who give.

Then there was the neighbor whose wife is leaving him for another man. And the college kid came by. Defensive. Afraid. Confused. And angry with me and everyone else who is in the establishment. He's smoking pot. Not sure I really helped either one of them.

But thanks for sending them my way.

And there is Stan in the hospital. Waiting surgery for a bad cancer. He's trying to adjust to the thoughts of dying. Patricia is there with a new baby. Her firstborn. And Eloise is in the hospital again. She changes doctors every six months. She is really mentally sick and needs help.

Doctor Gatlin stopped me to talk about the election. His wife has left him too. He's a good guy. And I pray for Mrs. Partin, the nurse. Her husband is not working again.

Thanks for the opportunity to help someone there.

Jarris called. He's drunk again. Jim came by. His Sunday school class is growing. He's a good man. Late afternoon meeting about a political campaign. I'm definitely interested in this Christian candidate. Two deacons at the house when I got home. Good men. They're going to ride with me to the revival. Two hundred miles to drive and a sermon to preach.

The children are asleep. I'll jot down some undone chores, say this prayer, and to bed. Good night, Lord.

Thank you.

THE PURPLE PLUM

FATHER, when I came in tonight and looked up at the church building site I saw the purple plum tree. Funny about that.

An angry, roaring fire destroyed our church buildings. It burned two big buildings. Pews. Organ. Hymnals. Everything burned. The flames also burned two big pin oaks. Magnolia. A dozen evergreens. Flowering crabs. Beautiful dogwoods. And a giant oak tree that was old and majestic lost its life in the fire.

But the little purple plum survived.

Then they came in to clean up the debris. They used cranes, trucks, bulldozers, trucks. A couple of times as many as two hundred men worked to clean up. They weren't too careful and other things were broken and destroyed.

But the purple plum survived.

Now they are building a new building. It is big. Expensive. They run bulldozers. Grade the lot. Dig a basement. Pour concrete. Dig sewer lines. And there is traffic, trucks, and more trucks. It's really hard to believe how much of a mess is made.

But the little purple plum still stands.

Maybe there is a parable here, Lord. I don't know that much about trees. Or about fires and bulldozers. Why can one tree stand the heat, and the digging, and the weather when others die?

It is true of people too. Some can stand the heat and others can't. It may be roots.

If so, help us plant our roots deeper. Like the purple plum.

JOLLY GEORGE

FATHER, I'm confused tonight. If anyone were to conduct a popularity contest in our church, everyone would probably think of jolly George. But they wouldn't vote for him. A couple of years ago he would have won a contest like that. Everyone liked him then.

George was loud, but not boisterous. He was a practical joker, but never hurt anyone. He was capable of sincere and compassionate interest. George was around when people had trouble and he brought optimism and hope to some of the most dismal situations. He was a tonic to drooping spirits.

But George changed. He changed suddenly. Dramatically. Oh, he still attends church. He is always around. But George has quit teasing. Quit laughing. Quit helping people. He is cross. Irritable. Glum. Cynical. Critical.

I don't know too much about people, but I decided George must be sick. But he wasn't. Maybe he had problems at work. He didn't. Fussing with his wife? No. Mad at the preacher or other church members? Not really. Finally I concluded that George was guilt-ridden. Something had happened that was bugging him. Something intense. Embarrassing. Something that George couldn't get over. And it was ruining his happiness.

For nearly two years I've tried to get next to George. I've tried to love him. To overlook his bad ways. To forgive his surly remarks. To help him find his old ways of happiness.

Today it all broke. George has been involved in a

financial scandal. He is to be indicted. He has apparently been guilty of fraud. I guess George is a crook.

So now what do I do? I was right. George was feeling painful guilt. But he waited and brooded and didn't correct his mistakes. Can George ever be happy again? I hope so, Lord.

MY HOME TOWN

FATHER, I went back to my home town today. A little county seat town in Kentucky. Funny how easy it was to recall things I thought had slipped away.

There used to be street lights hanging over the streets. We played baseball, shot marbles, and told stories under the lights. And bats swooped mysteriously by the light.

A big weeping willow tree made a tent for games of cowboys and Indians. We climbed the huge beech trees and stopped to smell lilacs. Occasionally we swiped violets and sold them to earn money for a coke. Once a million bees swarmed in a tree in a neighbor's yard.

The courthouse square hasn't changed much. We tossed a ball on the courthouse yard. Farmers sat on the benches on Saturday afternoon and swapped yarns while their wives shopped and exchanged gossip. There aren't many farmers left.

There was an old black man—Ed. He had a team of white horses. He would put a disc and a plow on a sled and go all over town fixing the gardens. I don't know what Ed did the rest of the time. I just remember the spring plowing.

The church bell rang on Sunday morning. Everyone could hear it. Not that everyone went to church. We walked to church and usually some of my cousins walked with us.

The town isn't really as I remember it. Maybe it never was. It's hard to know how memory and nostalgia mingle.

But I'm glad, Father, that there is some place that I can call a "Home Town."

THE WEDDING

FATHER, the wedding today is on my heart. I have known both of those kids since they were little. They should not have married. They are not ready. They won't make it. They didn't even want to marry.

She is pregnant. He is the father.

But marriage requires more than pregnancy to justify it. Giving birth to a baby doesn't make a mother. Marriage ceremonies don't build houses. Weddings don't establish families.

It's all wrong. Out of focus. Kids can't handle sex. Our sex education programs in schools and churches are failing. Parents must join us. The kids are getting the wrong information apparently. At least too many end up pregnant.

Then parents decide marriage is the best answer

to a difficult problem. They want to save face. They talk about giving the baby a name. As if any name will do. As if saving face is ultimate. As if a wedding ceremony makes it all right.

So I went along. What else to do? I tried to get her to go away. She could give the baby for adoption to someone who really wants it. Give the baby a chance and give the unprepared parents of the baby a chance.

But no one agreed. If I wouldn't marry them, they would go to a justice of the peace. Maybe they should have.

I just don't know what my proper role is in this kind of thing, Lord. But it happens more frequently.

We need something special from You.

A WEIGHT WATCHER

FATHER, I'm too fat. Not like a circus clown. Not the subject of jokes. Not blubber. Not short of breath and too awkward to walk.

But I carry too much weight for the pace I keep. When I lose a few pounds I feel better physically. Don't get as tired. Sleep better. And even function better. And it's always a morale boost to be able to shed some pounds by exercising self-discipline.

And overweight bugs me. Maybe it's the publicity about obesity and heart disease. Coronary. Choles- terol. Stroke. High blood pressure. Or it may be vanity about a paunchy belly. Double chins. Sagging chest. Flabby legs.

Really, though, I think its the question of self-discipline. I know I can lose weight by watching my diet and by not eating between meals, especially those late night snacks. It doesn't take long for me to lose the extra weight.

This is just a small thing. At this point weight isn't a serious health problem. As far as appearance is concerned, I'm not about to win any contests fat or slim. But it does disgust me that I don't have enough self-control.

About the only thing I can say about it is that my difficulty as a weight watcher has given me some sympathy, toleration, and understanding of other people who have their own problems of self-control.

Lord, I guess this is what You meant about picking sticks out of other people's eyes when there are pieces of lumber in our own.

FISHING

FATHER, my dad went fishing today. He has been retired for more than ten years. He is getting older. Health isn't too good but he doesn't complain much. Drives his car. Attends church. Watches ball games. But most of all, he enjoys fishing.

When I was a little boy I went fishing with him. Up at dawn. Out to some lonely creek in the country. Quiet. Cobwebs. Birds singing. The soft music of the stream. All day long we would fish. Not much conversation.

I never really liked to fish, and since I'm older and

busy I never go. Living in the city complicates it for me.

Dad fishes because he enjoys the out-of-doors. Looking at the sun rise. Watching a leaf fall. Birds building nests. Water bugs racing on the pond. A new wild flower blooming. Squirrels chattering.

There apparently is a challenge to fishing. Trying to outwit the fish who tries to outwit the fisherman. It's a question of survival for the fish and he will fight for his life.

I think the sincere fisherman likes the solitude best. In some way he finds the loneliness of fishing necessary. He thinks. Sits. Watches. Walks. Maybe he prays.

For years I've watched my dad go fishing and return. He always goes with eagerness and anticipation. He returns with some kind of reassurance, whether he catches fish or not.

Lord, maybe we all need to fish. At least we need something like fishing to offset our frantic living.

PATSY

FATHER, what will we do about Patsy? She is in a jam again, or better put, she is still in a jam. Patsy is a moral moron. She stays in trouble. She lives by no rules. She was and is man-crazy. Irresponsible. Indefensible. Immoral.

I've known her for a long time, Lord. I knew her before she got married and I've heard her repent and confess a dozen times.

She keeps getting messed up with men. She is cute, likable, and is constantly on the prowl. And there is always some fellow around to pick her up.

It's not that I feel so sorry for her husband— although I guess I should—but it's Patsy we need to help.

I realize she grew up in a bad home environment. Her mother and father separated. Her mother was busy trying to find a new husband. She never taught Patsy much and disciplined her even less. Patsy never learned much in school but she knows how to look good and how to talk to men.

And her husband is a misfit. At least he is for her.

Now she has come back to talk to me again. I don't know what to tell her, Lord. She has barnyard morals and romantic illusions about every man she meets.

My only hope is that time will bring a change. Maturity. Realism. And she does stay in church. As long as she stays in church, maybe we can help.

God, help Patsy. Our "Woman at the Well."

GENE

FATHER, when we were nine Gene and I went into Scouts together. Didn't surprise anyone, because Gene and I fished together, tramped through the woods together, played marbles together, and sat together in school.

Then we joined the church together. I pitched and he was the first baseman on the ball team. We double dated.

Today his mother called to tell me Gene is dead. Automobile wreck.

You know, Lord, I haven't seen him even one time in more than a dozen years. The last time I saw him he had changed. He was fat, loud, and a bore. He was trying too hard to impress me with his accomplishments. It wasn't a pleasant visit. I tried to recall some experiences from yesterday, but he wasn't interested. He wanted to talk about his work, his money, and his lady friends.

It was hard—impossible—for me to find my boyhood friend inside that loud mouth. Somewhere in his folds of fat and behind his obscene mouthings, the boy must be hidden. But he was hidden successfully.

Now he is dead.

I have tried since she called to sort it out. What happened to the boy? Where did he go? How do the passing years change a quiet boy into a vulgar, repulsive braggart? What makes a boy like Gene into such an obnoxious man?

Well, Lord, she wants me to preach his funeral. About all I can remember now is the man. Help me by funeral time to remember the boy.

A BOY AND HIS FRIENDS

FATHER, you don't have to live long to grow away from your friends of childhood. When I watch my own son with his buddies I invariably remember the boys I played with. We climbed trees. Fished. Played baseball. Read comic books. Wrestled.

We fought wild Indians. Built forts. Dammed up the creek. Walked in the woods. Caught fireflies, even bumble bees. Shot B.B. guns. Rode sleighs in the winter. Ate green apples. Played football. Whittled.

I don't remember that we talked a lot. We probably did, but the talking didn't make any lasting impressions on me.

We understood one another. We knew that some of the guys were poor. Others seemed to be rich. We knew that some were smart in school, others were slow. We knew that some of the boys had good parents, others had it pretty rough at home.

Because we knew all this, we didn't talk about it. You don't discuss money or arithmetic when you're building a tree house.

Somehow it was all easy, this business of being friends. We had our quarrels and usually settled them with a fist fight. Torn shirt. Bloody nose. Sore knuckles. But when the fight was over the quarrel was over.

There was a quiet quality of love about it all.

And now I'm older, Lord, and friendship isn't so quiet nor so easy. The growing up has made us all more suspicious, more devious, and less loving. In fact, not many of us even come close to the feeling we had as boys.

That's really a shame, Lord. We are missing something.

FIRST DAY OF SCHOOL

FATHER, pardon me for bothering You with such a little thing, but today my baby girl started school. It hit me kind of hard.

When she left this morning I could hardly believe it. She is so little. The school is so big. Walking away from the house, wearing new shoes and clutching a pencil, she was on top of the world. For weeks she has anticipated the day.

Excited. Unafraid.

We have passed a memorable milestone.

Never again will we have a little girl at home all day. Sometimes she slept late, sometimes she got up early. Talking to her dolls. Coloring pictures. Television blaring. A thousand questions. When I was working or reading she was always around, or at least it seemed that way. Now it will be quieter around the house. As if quiet houses are so important.

But this is all necessary and right. The little people must go out on their own. It's not just a question of learning to read and write. School is more than that.

It's the discipline of learning. Meeting children of different sizes, shapes, and colors. Exposure to the rich and poor. New people. Some will be kind, others will be tough. She will cry sometimes. And laugh a lot. Going to school is quite an adventure.

We will be here when she comes home. Listening to her stories. Sharing her achievements. Offering consolation in her disappointments. Looking at her homework. Loving her. And secretly wondering if the teacher knows how special she is.

Anyway, Lord, it's an important day at our house and I wouldn't feel right if I didn't talk to You about it.

TALK, TALK, TALK

FATHER, that ministers' meeting this morning bugged me. It was another one of these all-white conferences of preachers and priests. And as usual we "dialogued" about the blacks. But no blacks were there. This is about par too. Rarely do blacks come to meetings about the blacks. So we sit around and analyze the plight of the blacks, castigate the whites in general, and compliment ourselves for having the courage and compassion to attend this kind of meeting.

Lord, I'm sick of this kind of meeting. I'm tired of listening to pious white men sit around incessantly discussing blacks. So much of this kind of palaver is trite at best and sheer hypocrisy at worst.

I'm tired of blacks who complain, whine, and threaten, but who refuse to communicate in the most basic ways. A new kind of black separation is as offensive to me as white supremacy has been.

And I'm fed up with whites and blacks who spend their time verbally whipping the WASP. There are a lot of things wrong in race relations, but all of this placing blame isn't helping anything. Name-calling won't do the job.

Now it seems to me, Father, that men of good will should be able to bring something creative and courageous to this dilemma. Surely we can do something Christian and consequently helpful. Some significant answers can be found.

I think we all know where this Christian answer is, too. And it's not in conversation, criticism, or delusion. The answer is where it has always been. It's in imitating Jesus. Isn't that right, Lord? You want us to act toward other people, as Jesus acted down here.

Sorry I got mad today. But words without deeds get disgusting.

MR. ORVILLE

FATHER, it takes all kinds of people. Eventually we meet most of them, and if we pay attention with any kind of sensitivity we learn something from them.

Tonight I'm thinking about Mr. Orville. For the past six or seven years I've been hearing people talk about him. Everyone calls him Mr. Orville. He is rich. Inherited all kinds of cash and investment money from parents and grandparents. The money is in trust and the bank gives him an allowance of $100,000 a year to spend on himself. The bank manages his investments, his farms, and his business places. He doesn't know much about his wealth and doesn't care.

Today I met him and talked with him for a couple of hours. He is shy. Very self-conscious. He spends some money on custom-made automobiles. He had three custom-made cars in the garage. He travels to Europe at least once a year and collects things. His favorite collector's item is blue china. It's impossible to catalog the pieces of blue china he has.

I've been sitting here thinking, Lord. What would I do if I had $100,000 a year to spend on myself? Buy custom-made cars? I doubt it. Surely I wouldn't buy blue china.

Probably I would spend most of it on my children. Their happiness. Their education. Their security. The future. But Mr. Orville has no children. No wife. No living relatives at all. Custom Cadillacs and blue china are pitiful substitutes for children.

Honestly, Father, I believe I would spend some of it on the church, or missions. Some for the poor. The handicapped. The suffering. Some of it would go to preach the Gospel.

But Mr. Orville isn't a Christian, so he wouldn't know about that. And what does it profit a man to have $100,000 and lose his soul?

Please, Lord, help Mr. Orville.

A QUIET TIME

FATHER, everyone in America is talking about pollution. The streams are filled with bottles, paper cups, and sewage. The air is heavy and sticky. Trees die. Grass withers. Mountains erode. Roads are littered.

I know our planet is overcrowded. We are, in fact, corrupting the universe in a senseless, even dangerous way. Yesterday I read something about noise pollution and I've been thinking about that.

Maybe it's just selfishness. Maybe I'm just tired. But this noise thing pollutes my soul. Sounds. Sounds. Sounds. Screaming sirens. Roaring trucks. Humming and buzzing appliances. Blaring radios. Shouting voices. Television. Air hammers. Jet planes. Typewriters. Factory machines. Phones.

It's hard to find a quiet place or a quiet time.

Lord, I need it. We all need it. Quiet times when we can think. Or daydream. Or sleep. Or plan. Or pray. I remember some quiet times and places of another day, another generation. Was it ten years ago, or thirty years ago? Or was it ever?

I think I remember sitting beside a country stream. No planes. No trucks. No phones. Only the lapping water.. The whisper of a water bug. A swish of a butterfly. I think I remember midnight. Lying with another ten-year-old boy on a meadow hillside. Stars are silent. The moon makes no noise. We counted lightning bugs, but we didn't talk. Drifted off in a world of imagination.

And I try again to remember a snowfall. Was it last winter or a million years ago when the snow was so quiet and still?

Tonight I pray for a silent, quiet moment worth remembering.

GREED

FATHER, it is another case of greed. No one talks about it much anymore. But greed was once an embarrassing word. An ugly word. An obscene word. Greed meant lust. And selfishness. Dishonesty. Scheming and conniving. It said something repulsive. And it still says the same.

For a while greed can be camouflaged and covered up. It hides behind ambition. Enthusiasm. Cleverness. Shrewdness. It is costumed in self-interest and, what is even worse, it can be disguised in public service.

But like all evil it always shows itself. Eventually all of the façade is gone and evil—greed—is there. Naked. Uncovered. Still ugly.

I'm upset tonight, Lord, over two things. I'm sick about those people in politics, religion, and education who use other unsuspecting people for their own greed and selfishness. They dupe the innocent. Betray trust. Misuse confidence. They tell people their projects are for the public good, or even worse—for Your Glory—and then they use their project to line their own purse. Their grimy, greedy fingers keep appearing. This irritates me, Lord, and it must anger You.

And while I'm at it—I'm burned up with people who try to use the church for their own greedy purposes. They join the church so they will get new business, or more business. Or they try to make points in popularity by using the church. Or they try to use church people in their sales operations.

You will have to pardon me tonight, Father, but I'm just disgusted with greedy people who use innocent people. Especially in Your name.

LUCILLE

FATHER, I was driving through this subdivision and saw Lucille sitting on the porch steps this morning. She looked rather disconsolate so I stopped to chat for a minute. She was feeling low. Her first and only little one started to school this week. That was a big thing for Lucille and made me remember that day when our youngest started to school.

This is the first painful step in the process of growth that takes our children away from us. Up until this day they are always at home. Sometimes under foot and in the way, but they are there. We get used to the sounds they make. We sense their presence. The house has an aura of electric excitement (or is it apprehension?) when they are there.

Then they start school. And you worry and wonder, will they be safe? What if they get sick? Will the teacher be patient enough? Will they learn? Are they really old enough to go to school? Will bad kids influence them? Should you go with them the first day? Or any day?

No, it's not easy to send your child off to school. And in a fleeting thought you know this is one of a series of send-offs. Off to camp. Off on the first date. Off to college. Off to war. Off to their own wedding.

But this is the way it must be. They must grow and become persons in their own right. They must learn reading, writing, and arithmetic—and they must learn responsibility away from us.

So I pray for Lucille, and all the Lucilles when school starts. And I pray for myself. But I guess You understand about sending off a child.

RALPH

FATHER, I wish everything in the church could be easily defined. There should be some clear-cut, black-and-white answers. Some people always seem to be able to make that kind of decision. It's not always that easy for me. Especially when I'm dealing with people.

The one that's bugging me tonight, Lord, is Ralph. You know him as well as I do. He's a strange guy. He drinks. Uses bad language. Has been in prison. Chases girls. No one has respect for him.

But Ralph keeps coming to church. And that's the way it should be. People with moral problems like Ralph should come to church. That's what church is all about. At least we say that is what church is all about. We say that sinners like Ralph should come and worship with sinners like me.

He has a little boy and a drab little wife. I feel sorry for them. But they love him. He doesn't give them much of a home; he can't hold a job. And he doesn't give them any self-respect. They are poor and don't have many friends. Except a few people at the church who try to be friends. But the little boy and his wife love him.

The problem is that Ralph has started hanging around our youth group. I think he is a kind of hero to these kids because he has been in prison. He's a bad influence on the kids. I don't want those young people influenced or impressed by a guy like Ralph. They don't need to learn his tricks or imitate his style. He is worse than a loser.

But how to handle it? We can't throw a guy like

Ralph out. Maybe he does want help. Maybe he is sincere. Maybe he will change; at least we're in the life-changing business. And his wife and little boy love him.

You do too, Father, so help us all.

AT NIGHT

FATHER, as You know I stay up pretty late at night and get up early in the morning. Too little sleep wears me out, but there is a kind of mystery to those quiet times. And I'm thankful for them. For those minutes after midnight and at dawning.

Outside on a summer night the stars are always brighter, the moon more light. I can't really believe that men have walked on the moon. It's quiet on my street. Occasionally I hear the sound of a big truck on the highway or a siren crying out in the stillness. Mostly the sounds are not noticed, unless you tune in to hear them. Night sounds are so familiar that their silent symphony is unheard.

And You know that somewhere in the city a policeman is making an arrest, a surgeon is operating on a patient, a mother is giving birth, a nurse is standing by a bed. Somewhere in those quiet moments a man is lying awake worrying over a problem, another pacing the floor. A man is dying in a bed. A young couple is quarreling and saying harsh things. But for the most part the city sleeps.

Fireflies move slowly across the lawn. A dog wanders aimlessly past the bushes, followed in step by our neighbor's old cat. An evening breeze cools off the August night and the bird sings out to his mate. And I wish I was a poet or a songster and could capture the feeling of quietness to hold against the clang and clamor of the waking and working hours.

In the house my children sleep the innocent sleep of children. Sheltered and secure. Loved and contented. Peaceful and unafraid. Fed and clothed. Precious children. Boys and girls are entitled to quiet sleep.

God, grant them this in their childhood. Sleepless nights of unrelieved worry, unsought pain, and undone work all come soon enough. Give them some more nights of innocent sleep.

GETTING ATTENTION

FATHER, so much of what we do and say is designed to attract attention. Babies learn this immediately and so they bawl and yell and we pick them up. Problem is that most of us continue all our lives this baby pattern of making noise to be noticed.

I wonder sometimes about this need for attention. We try to act smart or smug. Dress in certain ways. Costume ourselves. Talk too much and too loud. Laugh at things that aren't funny and cry when we don't feel sad, just to get attention. Some of us preen like peacocks and make noise like hyenas just to be noticed.

Seems like this goes much deeper and has a more profound effect on a lot of other people. Kids, for instance, break the law, defy authority, behave in shocking ways, run in gangs, and get into trouble in some pitiable attempt to get attention. It works. They are noticed.

And some others—not just kids—develop illnesses. Headaches, backaches. Stomach aches. A dozen kinds of pain and sickness. They take pills. Go to doctors. Lie in bed. Mope around. And describe their illness in detail. All in an attempt to get attention.

Yes, Lord, it seems that we're capable of all kinds of bizarre behavior and conduct just to be noticed by others. Maybe we feel unloved. Misunderstood. Anxious. Afraid. Insecure.

It's this kind of thing that drives some people to suicide, I guess.

But remind us, Father, that we don't have to do all these things to get Your attention. You can even number the hairs of our heads.

AT 4:00 A.M.

FATHER, I was sitting in the hospital waiting room yesterday morning at 4:00 A.M. I've been there before and there is always something peculiar and memorable about a hospital so early in the morning.

Of course no one would be sitting there at 4:00 A.M. unless something is wrong with a loved one. Something terribly wrong. Wrong enough that you sit up all night. Anxious. Reflective. Afraid. Tense.

Hospitals have a certain sound at 4:00 A.M. The sloshing of a mop as an old man cleans the floor. The nurses' hurrying steps as they go from room to room and look in on sleeping—or awake—patients. The murmuring conversation from the nurses' station. Occasionally you hear them laugh and you wonder how anyone can laugh when you are so worried. You hear the automatic and regular sounds of oxygen and breathing machines and other mechanical equipment that keeps people alive.

Out of the reverie you begin to talk to the other man in the waiting room. Until now you have never seen him before. You have nothing in common. Under normal circumstances you would have little to talk about. But at 4:00 A.M. in a hospital room you meet on common ground. The level places of pain and fear. And you draw comfort from one another. It is as if you were old friends. And had been friends forever.

Early that dawning his wife died. He left to go away with his own family. With those he has known forever he will wear out his grief and get his help.

Funny now, but I didn't even learn his name. But for a couple of hours he and I talked, and by our talking we each drew from the other. Maybe in that way You too were in the room 4:00 A.M.

Bless that man, Father.

BROTHER JOHNSON

FATHER, I went to this celebration the other Sunday for Brother Roy Johnson. A church honored him in a special way for his fiftieth anniversary as a preacher. It was impressive to me and to everyone else who was there.

There were a lot of things that were impressive. He has spent his entire fifty-year ministry in one locality. He has been pastor of five churches during that half century, all of them within twenty miles of one another. That says a lot about his reputation. Many preachers couldn't get called to a church within two hundred miles of their present assignment.

He has married nearly two hundred couples, conducted about that many funerals, and baptized several thousand. Although that's statistics, it also represents people. We don't know how You keep score, but I think You keep score by people, not numbers.

Anyhow, this was all personal to me. He baptized me when I was eleven, and seven years later I left home as an ordained preacher myself. So he was the only pastor I've ever had. People who know us both say that I learned to imitate him in many ways when I began preaching. I hope so.

I think I was most impressed at this celebration with the genuine affection people showed him. They hugged his neck. Kissed his cheek. Wept when he wept. Laughed at his jokes. Touched his hands kindly. He is a man of strong and open feelings, and his friends and disciples respond with open feelings.

But You know all this, Father. You were there too. Of course You are usually around where Roy Johnson is. Thank You for him.

SPEAK, LORD

FATHER, why do so many things in life require such difficult decisions? Sure, some things are black and white. Clear cut. Easy to decide. Plain and simple. Not tough to know what to do in those experiences.

But more often than not, Lord, the issues are complex and confusing. There aren't always road signs and street lights. There are dark alleys and unmarked bridges. Invisible lines that we cross.

So we try to look ahead, to see into the future. I don't use crystal balls or read astrology tables or play games with fortune tellers, but I do something else that is foolish—I try to see the future based on my knowledge of the past. And this is always folly, because I see the future through my own prejudiced and self-centered focus. I try to decide what is at the top of the hill, around the curve, down the stream, and what is going to happen next Monday.

I also look back. I make decisions based on past experiences. The older we get, the more we tend to do this, I think. Looking back, trying to recall the circumstances and the factors that made us act or think or feel as we did.

So in some way we try to balance the past and the future and make a decision. But the decisions still come out stupid and selfish. At least they come out that way too often. Far too often.

This is exactly why I'm praying. You don't do stupid, selfish things. You know past and future. As it was and as it will be. You can help a fellow like me.

Speak, Lord.

THINGS NO ONE WANTS

FATHER, I've been thinking today about some of the people in our church who spend a lot of time trying to sell things to people that the people don't really need and don't really want to buy. Having never been a salesman, I'm not sure how it works, but it is a tough project.

They have to create the illusion of need and make the potential customer believe the product is necessary or useful. Most of the time they try to make people believe that others use the product and are happier, prettier, healthier, or wealthier for using it.

Not that there is really anything immoral about this kind of business. I don't suppose it is a question of right or wrong. Surely the customer has the right to say no.

But I believe it does something to salespeople. They lose some sense of dignity and worth. They don't feel their occupation is important. That what they are doing makes any difference. It's all transitory and changing. It doesn't last. They make money, but they don't make any changes. Often they don't make any friends either.

Maybe the word is integrity.

A man needs to feel that what he does reflects what he is. He needs to know that his occupation is a reflection, that it mirrors his character. His work should be an extension of his personal goals and personal commitment.

Those who just want money, can find it. Those who deal with things that aren't needed or wanted usually end up empty. Help them find some meaning in their work, Lord.

JULY 4TH—THANKSGIVING

FATHER, I'm glad to be an American. Grateful to You for the spacious skies, the golden grain, the purple-topped mountains. For this land that stretches from sea to shining sea. Grateful for roaring rivers and trickling streams. For coal and oil buried beneath the ground. For raspberries and walnuts. Mocking birds and robins. For wild flowers and tall trees.

Grateful for Jefferson and Franklin. Roger Williams. Valley Forge. For men who dreamed of freedom under God and came to this place to find it. Found it, only to lose it. Lost it, only to find it again. For men who wrote, spoke, persuaded, prayed, and even died to keep it. It's never been easy to be free. To be independent of tyranny. To believe, much less to practice, the equality of all with inalienable rights.

And I'm grateful to You for those who have preserved it for 200 years. The bluebloods, farmers, lawyers, Irish, mountain men, cowboys, housewives, pioneers, riverboat captains, teachers, and politicians. The wars—senseless and cruel. The progress—slow but steady.

There is plenty wrong—abortion, drug abuse, rampant materialism and self-centeredness—but there is still more here to be thankful for than anyplace else in the world at any other time in history. So I'm going to have a special prayer on July 4th. You have been good to us, Lord.

MY TEENAGER

FATHER, it doesn't seem long ago that he was born. When he was little he used to ask questions about his birthplace and the house we lived in until he was two.

Sat on my lap. Wrestled. Tossed a ball. Went for walks. Asked and answered endless questions. Built tree houses. Collected rocks and fish. Knives and toy guns. Built models and played on the floor.

Now he has become a teenager.

His voice is changing. No amount of food fills him up. A few hairs on his chest. Sometimes he is conscious of his clothes. Blushes when we tease about girls. Closes the door to his room. Comes in moody and irritable. Wants to start the car.

But the change isn't complete. He still climbs the tree to the treehouse. Gets out the small toys (but puts them away if anyone comes). Isn't sure where the line between boy and man is drawn. He will kiss me good night—if no one is around.

Precious boy. Guide him, Lord, through these difficult and ecstatic days of growing up. I remember, how well I remember, every miserable and marvelous day of adolescence. Nothing like it.

How desperately I want to interfere. How urgently I want to advise. But please help me to keep out of it. To stand back where he can reach me when he needs me.

He's growing up and away. And that's how it should be. Help us both, Father.

FATHER'S DAY

FATHER, tonight I'm thinking about being a father—looking ahead to trying to preach a Father's Day sermon I guess. And I'm thinking of all the things that can't, won't, and shouldn't be said in a sermon.

Things like the secret ways you look at your children trying to find some of yourself reincarnated. Brown eyes. Crooked toe. Cleft chin. Slim figures. Mannerisms. The careful scrutiny of a proud papa trying to find something of himself in his child.

I'm thinking about the secret, never-spoken pride that a dad feels. No other child is as handsome or as smart. No other child is really quite as clever or cute. Pride even in their tears and lost fights. Pride even when their dreams are broken.

And I'm thinking of their unique, never-to-be-duplicated personalities. The way they laugh and the way they pout. The things they collect that are meaningful to them—dolls, blocks, knives, baseball gloves, soldiers, coloring books, records, model cars, sewing sets, pictures on the wall—that vast collection they outgrow and put away, and which one day I miss because it is all gone. Forever gone.

This brings me impulsively to prayer. For I know that this wonderfully exciting business of being a father to children at home ends all too soon.

Excuse me, Lord, as I slip in and kiss them good night while there is still time. While they are still home.

A COMMENCEMENT SPEECH

FATHER, it's that time of year again. Commencement season. Thousands are graduating from high school and college. And it's my privilege to speak to some of the graduating classes.

Not that the kids pay much attention to the speaker. I'm not vain enough to think that. I know they will be thinking about a million things while I'm delivering the address. Some of them are sentimental about the old alma mater. Some are afraid of the future. Some are eager and excited about a new lifestyle. Some are thinking about their date after commencement is over. Others are just bored with the entire ceremony.

It means more to the parents. In fact, many of the parents didn't get this far along in school. For a long time they have worked and prayed for commencement. They were determined that their kids would get the education they missed. And now they have mixed feelings. Pride. Reward. Accomplishment. They too are a little sentimental. The child is about to leave home for good. Some apprehension about the future. War. Riots. Crime. Marriage?

It means something to the teachers. Even to the most discontented and critical teacher. Something of the teacher's life is invested in each kid. The teacher's talent. Convictions. Knowledge. Time and energy. The teacher on commencement night may have the most acute and sincere feelings of them all.

So I'll try to speak to students, parents, and teachers and say something that will make a difference, hopefully something they will remember.

For that big assignment, I'll need Your help.

PATIENCE

FATHER, tonight I pray for patience with my children—who must be told the same thing one hundred times, who make noise when I want quiet, who are quiet and alone when I crave their conversation and affection, who insist on loving me when I'm busy and who ignore my love when they're busy, who seem to make endless demands on my schedule, my bank account, and my wisdom—but who have never demanded too much.

And for patience with my church people—who get into the most unbelievable problems through stupidity and sin, who show me kindness and respect that is neither expected nor deserved, who call at all hours for help I cannot give, who seem to expect miracles I cannot work and wisdom I do not have (yet who accept my own human weakness and frailty with benevolent charity); for patience with people who are inane, sometimes ridiculous, often boring (yet who demonstrate to me and others an indescribable kind of generosity).

And for patience with things I cannot control. I'm so filled with egotistic esteem that I try to manipulate everything to my will. And when the winds and rains don't obey my will, I become cross and contrary. Teach me that some things are beyond my control and give me the grace to accept them. Teach me when to row upstream and when to portage. When to advance, when to stand pat, and when to retreat.

Lord, teach me patience.

THE WIDOWER

FATHER, Harold came by to talk today. It's been nine months since his wife died. I really haven't talked much with him lately. He is usually at church and he seemed to be getting along pretty well with the three children. In fact, someone told me he had been seen with a woman, so I figured he was coming through his grief in good shape.

Apparently I figured wrong.

He says he can't get over the loneliness. No adult to talk to about taxes, the washer, the pin oak, the price of shoes. No one to laugh with. Sure the children laugh with him, but it's not adult humor. No one to worry with. You just can't tell your kids about the things that worry you. And no one to fuss with. Sure you correct the kids and try to discipline them, but a man and his wife have those tensions that are peculiar to marriage. No one to plan with or dream with. The future seems gray.

And he says that he is confused about being mother and father both. It's hard to help a little girl shampoo her hair and to pick out shoes for her. And the boys don't keep their room clean. Washing and ironing can be done, and cooking too—but it isn't quite right. And it's more than household chores. The children miss the gentleness and love their mother brought to the family.

Religion helps, according to Harold. He hasn't lost any faith in You and he sticks pretty close to the church and his religious convictions. But he is a lonely widower. So far time is healing the hurt slowly. So I pray for Harold. Help him to heal more quickly.

UNITY

FATHER, I've been working in the church long enough to know that church people don't always get along with one another. Yet we are always surprised when other Christians get mad at one another, pick at one another, and cause dissension and discord.

When this kind of thing happens people outside the church hop into the hassle with both feet and use this as an excuse for their own unconcern about Your church. And there is a legitimate reason for the outsiders' criticism. Nothing is as mean and embarrassing as a church fight.

But, Lord, correct me if I'm wrong. Seems to me that we have overpromised in this area. We try to act like there's something magical about church work. As if church work will inherently be free of human desire, human weakness, and human personality.

We try to get people who are in trouble at their job, who have a sick gall bladder, who owe too much money, who have disobedient children or nagging spouses to suddenly and mysteriously leave all that behind when they come to church. We even tell them to leave the "outside" world outside the church. Then we assume that in spite of lack of money, poor health, and family problems they can "all work together in peace and harmony." That's too much assuming.

Actually, church people get along pretty well together considering the diversities of their religious experiences, the complexities of their family lives, the infirmities of their health, and the confusions of their minds.

I pray that people might learn to come just as they are and that we might learn more about accepting them and to be less concerned about changing them. I need a good dose of this right now.

THE OLD MAN

FATHER, an old man called. Said he was seventy-four and needed a home. Seems that he's been living with a son, daughter-in-law, and four grandchildren for about two years. He's sick. Can't walk too well, gets dizzy, has failing eyesight. One arm is crippled up. But he insists he is not an invalid and doesn't need nursing care.

The son runs a computer. The old man told me how much salary he makes and about his eight-room house. He's real proud of the boy. Says his house is one of the nicest in town.

The son told the old man he can't live there anymore—they need the bedroom because each of the children is entitled to a private room. Two of the children have been sharing a room, and they want some privacy.

The old man says he understands. Part of growing up. When he was a boy, one of eleven kids, he found privacy out behind a haystack, in a barn loft, fishing in a lonesome creek, or squirrel hunting at dawn. He says kids can't find privacy like that today. And of course that's true.

He didn't aim to interfere with his son's family. He ate meals with them; he can't do much cooking because of his bad arm and dizzy spells. Had his own television and spent most of his time in his own room. According to him, he tried to stay out of their life as much as possible. He had never been sick in bed one day.

But the children want their own room. And he wants me to find him a place to room and board.

I called the son to see if they couldn't build a room on the house for the old man or the kid who wants privacy. He says he can't afford to build a room.

So, Lord, help the old man, the son, and the child who wants privacy.

THE EXPERT

FATHER, I've known Pauline for quite a while. Ten years at least. She's one of those opinionated women who is an expert on everything. She is always telling someone when to buy groceries, when to plant flowers, how to fix her hair, how to save money. In any conversation Pauline interrupts and eventually dominates the discussion.

This all carries over into religion too—as You know. She has the last word on biblical interpretations. She always injects her opinions into church business. She is pious about her humility. She seems to be sure that You run a straight line to her waiting ear. People in the church don't think much of Pauline.

Pauline and her husband don't have children, but she constantly advises parents on when to feed a baby, how to correct a six-year-old, spank a ten-year-old, or counsel a fourteen-year-old. She believes the biggest problem in our world is the breakdown of family life.

And of course her dominant personality rules her husband. Actually he is a pretty decent guy. Most people like him, but people rarely invite George and Pauline to their home. He used to go fishing, but she decided it was bad for his health. And staying up late to watch ball games was bad for him too. However, if there is anything Pauline can expound on, it's the key to a happy marriage.

But, Lord, I just got this phone call. George has left Pauline. He wants a divorce. I have to go see her and I don't know what to say. Maybe for once, she doesn't know what to say either.

So I'll pray for George, and Pauline.

A LONE DAFFODIL

FATHER, it's been a long, dreary, snowy, and depressing winter. Winter isn't always a matter of climate and coldness. Often it is a matter of attitude and emotion. Of long days and slow mornings. Of dark skies and dull sunrises. Of wet shoes and red noses. Of silence.

Funny. The first daffodil I saw this spring was beside the road. Really at the end of a street in a residential area. Yellow. Brave. Bright little flower.

Ironically, all around the daffodil were tin cans, grocery bags, plastic wrappers. Garbage. Trash.

Someone had been using the end of the street as a private garbage dump. Maybe to avoid paying a garbage collector. Maybe out of thoughtlessness and carelessness.

But the garbage is vulgar. It is an obscenity. A shocking mess. It is smelly, out of place. Garbage should be hidden, destroyed. It should not be scattered.

I guess there is some parable in the daffodil amid the garbage. Proves that lovely things can grow in a bad environment. That thought encourages me, makes me hopeful. Especially after a long winter.

Actually daffodils are lovelier when they are together. When they are planted, watered, and cared for.

Help us to plant flower gardens, Lord. To give attention to lovely things. To look at beautiful things. To water and care for growing things.

But also help us to get the garbage and trash out of sight. To do our best to give daffodils a chance to grow.

JUST WHAT WE NEED

FATHER, I was listening to a song awhile ago. It says we can trust You—that You know just what we need. And that what we need and what we want aren't always the same.

Most of us go through life in a kind of reckless race trying to get the things we want. Things we can gain or buy. Things that are bought and sold. Things that improve our status and standing.

All of the time we have an awareness that what we really need isn't found in the marketplace. It isn't in toys and trinkets. It isn't bought or sold, measured or counted. It isn't touched and tasted. It isn't in what other people think of us, either, nor in what we think of ourselves, although both are important.

More than anything else, it seems to me, we are looking for people to love us just as we are. People who love us with our imperfections and handicaps. People who accept us. People who need us. People who understand us. People who don't expect us to be more than we can be. People who forgive us.

Lord, I can think of a hundred people right now who want to be loved. And I'm one of them. Now I don't doubt for a minute that You love us. This is the basis of this prayer, of any prayer. If You didn't love me, prayer would be empty. But there are a lot of loveless people who never pray. Help me find them. And to love them.

THE UNWED FATHER

FATHER, too many times a couple of kids have called me just like these two did. I'm beginning to recognize their tone, their deference and hesitancy, their embarrassment—they are expecting a baby. They have talked about it and decided to get married. And they want me to perform the wedding ceremony. When they come into my office they blurt it out. They want to get married right away. One small problem. They're both under age, so their parents will have to know so they can sign the papers.

The girl is from our church family. Pretty. Bright eyes. Sixteen. She is too young to get married and has no business with a baby. In fact, she hasn't been responsible for anything before. Spoiled at home. Indifferent at school. I cannot imagine her as a wife or mother. But I can tell by looking and listening— she does most of the talking—that she wants a husband. She wants this boy to marry her. The baby isn't a reality to her. A wedding and a husband are first in her mind. She isn't upset about her parents or her reputation or morals and religion—or about the baby or the boy. She just wants to be married.

I drew out of the boy some of his history. He is a football player; works as a carry-out boy in a supermarket. His parents don't have much. He had three or four scholarship offers to small colleges. He would like to study architecture.

He is quiet. Embarrassed. Really doesn't want to get married. Probably doesn't like the girl very much. Knows that he can't do much for the girl or the baby. Once he looked me full in the face. Most of the time he looked at the floor. I guess at this point he is only capable of looking down.

Poor boy. I pray for him. And the girl. And the baby.

LISTENING

FATHER, this teenage boy was back in today. He is a restless, unhappy, confused fellow. Can't get along with his parents, doesn't have many friends, does poorly in school, and is mixed up about religion. He's talked with me three or four times, but I'm at a loss.

Apparently there is no single thing that bugs him. He doesn't pin down any particular kind of problem. It's not that his parents are mean to him. He has money to spend. He is sharp enough to learn in school. Attractive enough to make friends.

His pitch is that no one really pays any serious attention to him. No one seeks his opinion or asks his advice. No one listens to what he is saying. Consequently he has quit talking and reverts to sulking in silence. And of course this complicates his problems.

It seems to me, Lord, that this thing of listening to other people is a complexity of our time. It is not peculiar to the younger generation. The same thing happens between husbands and wives, doctors and patients, coaches and athletes, conductors and musicians, bosses and employees, politicians and voters.

There is enough sound. But it's not easily interpreted or understood. Too much sound and too few who listen.

No one should realize this more than a preacher. We say the right thing at the right place and at the appointed time. But too few listen.

Well, back to the boy. I don't have answers for him, but maybe just listening to him will help for a while.

And this whole business of praying has something to do with Your listening to our sounds.

SPIRITUAL THINGS

FATHER, they had this telerama here last week for the March of Dimes. Left me with some mixed feelings. Some of the entertainers and others on the program kept talking about helping in the fight against birth defects as a religious obligation. Maybe they're just using religion to help promote their favorite charity.

On the other hand, a preacher told me he didn't give money to things like the March of Dimes because he gave his money for spiritual things. Said his church didn't support social causes because they were interested in spiritual causes.

Well, I happen to know some of the kids affected and afflicted by birth defects. A little boy without feet, a blind two-year-old girl, a twenty-one-year-old boy who is deaf and mute. And there are more than thirty mentally retarded kids in our Sunday school. All these kids kept popping up in my mind when this preacher was talking about spiritual things.

And I tried to think about Jesus. He said that He came to do what You sent Him to do. In fact He claimed to have done what You sent Him to do. That was a bold statement. Somehow He did it though. In fact He ended up on a cross for that very reason.

Anyhow, Lord, I just can't imagine Him telling a crippled, blind, retarded, sick, or deaf child that He was only interested in spiritual things. Seems like He was always interested in children with all of their afflictions and problems.

Well, thinking about Jesus made us contribute to the March of Dimes. And we feel right about it. I'm really praying for all of us to discern what is really spiritual.

OVERFLOW

FATHER, I guess every well runs dry. And there is a limit to every bank's total deposits. There is no way we can keep dissipating our emotional resources without adding some.

In other words, I'm drained.

More and more the preacher spends time with people who are in trouble. Sickness. Death. Broken laws. Broken homes. Broken hearts. Broken bodies.

The real problem for me is overflow. We need enough extra in our emotional reservoir to spill over to those who need help.

Not that any preacher has too much or even enough courage in the face of adversity. Enough strength to combat weakness. Enough grace to conquer crudeness. Enough faith to move mountains. Or enough love to include the whole world.

But we all have some of these virtues. And our burden is to keep enough built up to be able to effectively and successfully share with others in obvious and dire need.

Teach us the joy of sharing and deliver us from a miserly attitude. Teach us the joy of giving and deliver us from hoarding. Teach us the satisfaction of fatigue and deliver us from laziness.

While we are learning, multiply and enlarge our capacity for overflow. Grant us enough love and discipline that our spiritual resources will be unlimited and our desire to share will be unchecked.

May something good spill over from our own cup of joy.

WHY?

FATHER, I heard about it on the radio. Newscaster said a man had shot his wife. Her condition was serious, but she had told police her husband was the one who had shot her. They were looking for him. The newsman didn't give any names. They had found her in the parking lot of a shopping center. It was about 10:00 P.M.

They released the names on the eleven o'clock news. They had found the man. He had shot himself in the head. His condition was critical.

I knew them. They had attended our church.

When I got to the hospital he was dead. The police suggested I go with them to tell his wife. The officer said it would be hard for her. He said that women were funny, they would break up over something like this—even though the guy had tried to kill her.

The policeman was right. She took it pretty hard.

Today I conducted a funeral for him. Didn't know him very well. But I learned some things You had known. He was an alcoholic. Had served two prison terms. Had been married three times. Had shot one of his other wives. Apparently he was a confused, violent, driven man.

Tonight I'm wondering about this kind of man.

What goes into his make-up? What makes a quiet, rather insignificant looking fellow such an explosive package of uncontrolled feelings?

Could I have helped him? Could anyone have helped him? What was he saying when he came to church? What was he expecting that he didn't find? Do Christians have the answers for this kind of man?

I have a lot of questions tonight, Lord. If there are answers, You will have to give them.

DADDY WON'T LOVE ME ANYMORE

FATHER, this little girl lives on my street and plays with my little girl occasionally. In fact she is around the house more than occasionally.

Seems her dad is a pretty busy fellow. Gone from home a lot and doesn't have much time for the little girl. Like most parents he wants her to obey, to be clean, to be well-behaved.

She was saying the other day that she could not play in the snow because if she got her clothes wet her dad wouldn't love her anymore. And she said if she skinned her knee she shouldn't cry because if she cried her daddy wouldn't love her anymore. And she says that if she eats too much candy her daddy won't love her anymore. She worries about a missing tooth because her daddy might not love her anymore.

All of this gets to my little girl. Before long she is saying, "Daddy, do you love me?" or "Do you love me when I spill my milk?" or "Do you love me when I cry?" or "Do you love me when I break a toy?"

I don't know this man up the street very well, but I think he is way off center. Threatening a child by withholding love strikes me as being all wrong. Sure, kids must obey and honor their parents, but obedience can't be won by dangling love on a Yo-Yo.

Help us to let our kids know we love them all the time. Broken tooth. Crying. Skinned knees. Spilled milk. These things don't affect the way we love our children.

Surely, Father, Your love for us isn't that conditional and erratic. Teach us, God, and help us to teach our kids.

TOO LATE

FATHER, I'm not really sure why Harry left his wife and two children. It was nine or ten years ago and the children were young—but old enough to miss him. Young, but old enough to be disappointed and eventually to become bitter. Young, but old enough to be hurt.

Harry went South. Got a new job and a new wife. Things weren't really any better for him. New town, new job, new wife, but the same old Harry. Nothing was really different, so he left her. Went to Maryland.

He had been fairly active in church back here before he took off. In Maryland he got involved in church again. Apparently he settled down with another new job in another new town. Started sending me Christmas cards and occasionally he would write.

Last week he came back here. His daughter was getting married. I was to conduct the wedding. The girl is eighteen. Marrying a nice boy. They have made all the usual plans for a wedding. Florist. Photographers. Bridesmaids. Music. Reception. The works.

It never occurred to me that she didn't know Harry was back in town. In fact, I assumed he was here for the wedding.

He called me yesterday. He had called his daughter.

She had asked her uncle to give her away. She had never even thought of asking Harry to the wedding. No, she didn't expect him to attend. No, she didn't want him to be there.

Harry just called from the airport. He's flying back to Maryland.

He came home too late.

So I'm praying for Harry. And for his daughter, too.

THE CYNIC AND THE SNOW

FATHER, maybe this young man Gilbert is typical of young men today. I see him every week when I go to the television station to make the video tapes for our program.

It started during Christmas. He said he didn't send cards or exchange gifts. Said that Christmas was too commercial. I asked him if he thought it should be more religious.

"Not really," he said, "I don't think much of religion either."

Now I've found out that he doesn't pay any attention to the news, is unconcerned about social problems, sleeps through the State of the Union message, and couldn't care less about the local basketball scores.

But he operates a camera on a television news program. The news is of no interest to him. His only reason for being there is to focus the camera. He says he is a technician, not a commentator or even an observer.

I've never tried to preach to or argue with Gilbert. Every week I try to get him involved in some kind of conversation. He will talk. But it is all critical, cynical, and caustic. Nothing interests him. No excitement. No anticipation. No light in his eyes or warmth in his face. Frustrated. Coldly angry. Aloof and arrogant.

But today I found his soft spot. We had three inches of snow, and he talked like a poet about the soft, white crystals. The unmarked snowy dawn. And he talked about sunsets. April rains. Autumn colors. Spring flowers.

His eyes were warm. You got to him, Lord, with the wonders of nature.

SERMONS

FATHER, I guess we all are impressed with the sound of our own voice. With the logic of our own thinking. With the influence we have over the minds and conduct of others. This self-importance is a particular hazard to preachers. At least to this preacher.

Funny how we delude ourselves about this when our listeners really don't pay much attention to what we're saying. I've asked them to recall a sermon title or text and they don't remember from one week to the next. But they do remember a story, especially if it is funny or sad.

Sometimes when I preach and realize how little they are getting, I feel like quitting. Walking out. Giving up.

Oratory, logic, and eloquence seem lost in their preoccupation with personal problems, private prejudices, and disinterest.

Yet things do happen. Often at the least expected times and surely in the most unexpected ways.

Like today when Marie came by. She has decided to go on to school and become a worker with mountain poor. She has quit her job. Sold her new car.

She may not stick to it. But like Christy in Catherine Marshall's book, she has decided this is what You want her to do. I pray that You will help her in this decision and resolution.

And like Christy, she says she made her decision one Sunday when I was preaching. She said the sermon got to her.

I needed that. Thank You, Father.

CHESTER

FATHER, this thing with Chester is perplexing me. He is nineteen, over six feet tall, healthy—and mentally disabled. He has the mind of a seven-year-old.

Seems that Chester's mother deserted him when he was two or three. They couldn't find her, or if they did find her she didn't want Chester. He became a ward of the State. He isn't a threat to anyone's health or well-being, but he has been in more than a dozen different foster homes; no one keeps him long because he is a nuisance. He talks a lot. He paces the floor at times, preoccupied with a world of his own. So eventually they give him back to the State.

He goes to school and is learning. Slowly. But he is learning. He will probably be able to work some day as a dishwasher in a restaurant, perhaps as a bus boy.

Chester has never been in trouble, but he is easily influenced by other people because he is always anxious to win their favor. He will do what people tell him to do. He could steal just as easily as not.

Right now he is staying in a cheap hotel. The State pays the room rent. He has a little record player we gave him and he likes Tom Jones records. Yesterday we took him some food and a portable TV. At night some of us have been checking up on him.

We're trying to win his confidence. Chester is black. Someone taught him that white people will mistreat him, and so he is afraid of us. But we're making progress.

Lord, help Chester and help us to help Chester.

THE BORE

FATHER, I've just had another session with Russell Lee. I sense that something is wrong with him down inside. As far as I know he gets along with his wife all right and with his children. In fact he seems devoted to her and the two little girls.

But this guy always has a new project in mind. He has changed jobs a dozen times. He is always on the trail of some pot of gold. Always some new investment. Always some way to get ahead financially. Some new job.

It gets disgusting. He has no interest in what's going on in the world around him. He just talks and talks about his latest business venture or vocational experiment. He seems oblivious to people except as they relate to his work or as they listen to his conversation.

He doesn't have friends; people don't like him. They try to avoid him. I've never been rude to him, but maybe I should try to tell him what's going on.

Lord, what kind of obligation do we have to people like Russell Lee?

Should we allow them, without protest or advice, to go ahead in their self-centered way? They are bores. Friendless. Actually foolish.

Or is it presumptuous to interfere with a man like this? If he can't see it in himself, do I have any responsibility to tell him?

What about Russell Lee?

A POOR DRAMA

FATHER, every time I'm called on to conduct a funeral I feel my own inadequacy. Especially when I don't know the deceased, the family, or anyone else—and they don't know me.

The one today was like that.

What is especially poignant about this kind is that apparently no one else knows or cares either. Only seven people, in addition to the pallbearers, were at the funeral home today, even though the woman had lived in our city most of her life. Divorced. Two sisters were there, but their husbands didn't come. No children. No parents. No church.

They called me because they had heard me on the radio.

I don't think I helped anyone. Not that anyone there was really heartbroken. No one acted like they needed help.

They didn't seem to listen to what I had to say. And there wasn't too much to say. Nothing about the woman at least, because I didn't know her. Nothing much to the family—just these two unconcerned sisters. Everyone wanted to get it over with.

So we did. They called me because they needed a minister to make the service decent. A minister is as much a part of the death ritual as embalming, flowers, and driving to the cemetery with headlights on.

But it is still with me, Father. She was one of Your children and we will just have to leave this all up to You.

Me? I feel as if I've been an actor in a poorly

written and poorly produced drama that no one watched.

A NEW FATHER

FATHER, I've never seen a new father as excited as Johnny. Maybe it's only because I know him better than I know most new fathers. Perhaps I just caught him at the height of his exuberance and joy.

Anyhow, I want to pray for him as he begins the strange but delightful pilgrimage of fatherhood.

Give him the kind of moral courage he needs to teach this little boy right from wrong. Help him to act with confidence without being arrogant. Grant that the child will respect his father without expecting too much from him.

Give him a sense of humor. Don't let the seriousness of being a parent overwhelm him. He will have a lot of responsibility, but it will be fun as well as hard work. Grant that the little one will grow up laughing and that he will be able to laugh at himself, or at his parents.

Give him the ability to listen. The baby will soon learn to cry for attention, and there is a difference in crying for attention and crying because something hurts. As he grows older the thing that hurts the most will probably be this need for attention. Help his dad to hear not only the cries, but the whispers, the conversations, and the questions.

Give Johnny the ability to express his love for the child. To speak love. To show love by touch. By giving. Grant that Johnny and his new baby will learn the language of love.

Father, You can do all this for Johnny and all of his kind. After all You know what it's like to have a Son.

SIX CHILDREN

FATHER, most people call him "Chuck." But his wife calls him "Charles." Somehow neither name seems to fit. "Charley," I think, would be most appropriate, but no one calls him "Charley."

He is a strange one. Gentle and patient with his children. They adore him. He makes wise cracks with his kids. They share secret jokes and seem to have a good time. There are six little ones, and they all have his blond hair and brown eyes. He is a skilled carpenter. Really he is a woodworker, a craftsman.

But he drinks too much. Way too much. And this wastes his money, upsets his children, and keeps his wife on edge. When he is drinking he is loud, vulgar, and cross. He gets into fights. In jail. Wrecks cars. And when he is really drunk, he tears up the house, terrorizes the children, and beats his wife.

So after a long time we got Charley involved in church. He repented. Was baptized. Began attending regularly. Quit drinking. In fact he hasn't had a drink for more than six months. Says he feels like a new man. His kids are different. He's paying off some debts. Everything looks better. I know You had a lot to do with it.

My problem is his wife. She bugs him all the time.

Everything he does is wrong to her. Nag. Pick. Fuss. Quarrel. She calls me up with all of her inane and idiotic complaints. About to drive me crazy, and I really feel for old Charley.

Lord, I've decided it takes more of a miracle to change someone who is nagging and neurotic than it does to change someone who drinks too much. So I pray for Charley and his wife.

And especially for the six children. The real losers.

THE MAN WHO HAS EVERYTHING

FATHER, it's that time of year again. Christmas. Everyone is excited, busy—sometimes it approaches frenzy. And the advertisements are talking about buying unusual and special gifts for the man who has everything.

I keep thinking about that catchy phrase: "The man who has everything." They mean, of course, the man who has plenty of clothes, all the popular do-it-yourself gadgets, the best razors and golf clubs, the big cars. They mean the man who has a good job, big house, and the most expensive guns and tools. They're talking about Mr. Affluent American.

You and I both know the kind of man they mean. We know that it isn't always the way it looks.

I pray for the man who has everything—except a loving wife. Everything except a woman who shares his deepest longings and his most persistent fears. Everything but a wife who is actually a part of his life.

I pray for the man who has everything—except self-respect. He doesn't like himself. Guilt. Failure in his secret goals. Tired of materialism. He isn't what he ought to be and he knows it. This gnaws on him.

I pray for the man who has everything—except peace of mind. Restless. Anxious. Irritable. Afraid. He doesn't sleep well. Can't relax. Filled with tension. Always thinks that "something is wrong."

I pray for the man who has everything—and is afraid of losing it. He worked so hard, schemed so cleverly, collected so diligently, hoarded so carefully, and counts it so regularly. He has businesses, bowling trophies, shoes, books, degrees, influence, and a vault of money. But he spends his time worrying about losing any piece of it.

I pray for the man who has everything—except . . . ?

WHO WILL SEE THE TREE?

FATHER, I was out visiting today and stopped in to see an elderly blind woman who is a member of our church. I'm quick to admit that I don't visit her often enough; I realize how lonely she must be. But she doesn't seem to need me as much as some others do, because she knows You as well as anyone I know.

Inside her house was a nicely decorated Christmas tree; its lights burned brightly in the dim room. Most of the decorations were the old-fashioned type bulbs and globes. A few strands of tinsel. Silvery icicles. And a chain of shiny paper. It looked nice.

I admired the tree and asked her if she had decorated it herself. She said she always decorated her own tree. A nephew took her out to buy one as soon as they went on sale. In the "old days" she always had a tree brought in from the woods. She told me she always packed the decorations away in the same box and kept it in the closet in the same spot.

Decorating the tree is a big thing to her, even though she can't see it. She can't see the red, silver, and blue bulbs, the green tree, or the gold tinsel. She can't tell whether or not all the lights are burning or the bulbs are straight.

I wondered why she went to all that trouble. Going out to buy a tree. Decorating it with care. Putting it up early in a dim room. A blind woman with a Christmas tree? So I asked her, "Why do you go to all that trouble? Decorating a tree. When you're blind?"

And she said, "Why Reverend, everyone isn't blind."

A WRITER IN THE GHETTO

FATHER, I had dinner the other night with the editor of a religious magazine. He is the crusading type. Writes a lot about the poor, the handicapped, the minorities, and social injustice. Frankly he disturbs me by the intensity of his conviction.

Anyhow, he mentioned in conversation that he lives in a ghetto. That's right. He lives in the poorest section of his city. Moved there with his wife and kids. Says he wants to know first hand what it is like to live in the ghetto.

I can't get him out of my mind. Maybe he is just "grandstanding." Or perhaps his chosen lifestyle is a gesture. Or patronizing hypocrisy. Maybe he is just trying to make an impression or add authenticity to his writing. But his motives are Your business, not mine, so I'll have to leave the judgment with You.

Still, I'm troubled. He earns a good salary, has a fine education from an Ivy League school, has a wife and some sweet children, and no one asked him to do this.

Ghettos have their own stink. Garbage. Noise. Crime. Violence. Despair.

I've never lived in one. Probably never will. I've never even thought seriously about living there, although I've honestly tried to help some people who are. Tried to help them get out, or at least improve the place where they are trapped.

But this writer isn't trapped. On his own he went there to live. He chose it. He didn't have to go. Kind of sounds like the Christmas Story—You came down here, not because You had to, but because You wanted to.

Let me think on this awhile, Father.

HOW HIGH IS UP?

FATHER, while the astronauts were on the moon some people suggested to me that maybe some space traveler would find You there. Reminded me of the Russians who flew around in outer space and came back saying that they didn't see You "out there" so You must not be there at all.

All this space travel has put me to thinking. I talk to You, believe in You, and really don't doubt that You keep busy.

But I just can't picture You sitting on some planet or floating on a cloud or drifting around in outer space. I don't know what some think about Your geographical location, but I don't know, or don't worry a lot about, You being "up" or "out."

Seems to me that You tried to say something to us when You came "down" here. Seems to me that Jesus was all that You are. Walking in the sand, fishing in the sea, sleeping in the boat, crying at a grave, eating bread and fish, and loving His friends. Talking about forgiveness, turning the other cheek, and being kind to the needy.

And there was something mysterious and profound about the Cross, where You took on our pain, our hurt, our ugliness, our arrogance.

I suppose I never looked far beyond Jesus to find You. And I didn't really expect any space traveler to find anything about You "out there" or "up there."

How high is up? Lord, I've a feeling that we know as much about You in Jesus as we'll ever need to know.

Is that correct?

THE MINISTERIAL STUDENT

FATHER, I'm thinking tonight about Gary, the aspiring young preacher in our church. He's having a rough time. Needs some help that only You can give.

Entering the ministry has been tough for him. His family isn't particularly religious or church-centered. He doesn't know much about it. And in many ways he isn't learning much either.

Gary is a student at the University, which is part of his trouble. He struggles to make good grades. He is smart enough, but he isn't disciplined. And there aren't too many kids at the University who admire ministerial students. So they dig at him.

And he is confused about a lot of things. Life was much simpler when I was a ministerial student; the world was more calm.

Gary wants to preach because he has something to say. He wants to have an audience. He wants to see things changed. He wants to write. He wants to lead people.

But he is unsure. He hasn't grown enough to learn his audience. He isn't persuasive enough to change his listeners. He hasn't been at it long enough.

And he may give it all up first. That would be a shame, Lord, because he is sincere. Impetuous. Impatient. But honest. Help me to help him earn the place to speak.

SELF-RIGHTEOUS—WHO ME?

FATHER, I have a personal problem tonight. Most of the time I try to do what is right. Of course there are many times when I'm selfish, stupid, and tough on other people. And times when I flat-out do, say, and think things that are wrong. But that isn't my hang-up tonight.

It's so easy for me to become self-righteous. To assume that I have a corner on intelligence, insight, or moral persuasion. This is a professional hazard. People expect preachers to know right from wrong, to enunciate right and wrong, and consequently to act out the right decisions. They always think our conduct will reflect that kind of morality.

And when people expect it and want it that way, it's easy to decide it is true. That is the pitfall.

Preachers don't usually get put up on pedestals because of their wealth or power or appearance or education. Their precarious perch is based on their ability to moralize. Their prestige is rooted in the sandy soil of discrimination about right and wrong. People are anxious to find someone to decide for them what is right and wrong in the gray and fuzzy areas of life.

This is difficult; in fact, it is horrible. If we admit to people that we too have our doubts, our sins, our failures they are inclined to ignore us even when we speak with integrity and confidence. Yet we are the biggest fools on earth if we try to appear more righteous, more sure, more spiritual than we really are.

So I confess my own sin and failure to You. And I am willing, even anxious, to admit my sins to anyone else who will listen. I can't be an expert on being good.

PAT IS DEAD

FATHER, although I've been in the business of life and death for a long time now, there is still something awesome about death.

Now Pat is dead.

He moved to our city more than thirty years ago from down South. No relatives. Never married. He was a laborer and enjoyed telling about the buildings he had worked on.

Pat lived in one room in an old dilapidated hotel. Cooked on a hot plate. Watched a little TV at night. Before TV he listened to the radio. He had a few friends, but he was shy and, with no family, he was essentially alone.

A couple of our church members knew Pat. When he missed a week at his job—janitor in the Union Hall—they went to find him. He was sick in bed. Literally starving. Terribly alone.

We got him to the hospital. They fed him. Gave him tender loving care. Church people visited him, sent him cards, took him fruit, new pajamas—the first he had ever worn. We paid his bills. Prayed with him. The doctors gave him a complete check-up.

Cancer.

Now he is dead. For ten months we watched him die. Never once did he complain or whimper. He was so happy and glad for all his new friends. Lord, he was such a gentle man. In his case maybe sweet would be the word.

Father, I'm glad I knew Pat. And glad for the ones who found him in that room.

Is there another Pat in our city? Help us to find him.

THE SECOND TIME

FATHER, another wedding is over, but I was particularly impressed by this one.

It was quiet. No flowers. No wedding gown. No reception. No wedding march. No guests. No round of parties and showers prior to the wedding. The only relatives present were three small children. No professional photographer. They asked me to snap three pictures on their own camera.

They have both been married before. The first marriages didn't work. I didn't know why, but they were both anxious to explain it all to me. They both have children by the first marriage.

But the children aren't all that is left out of their previous marriages: they also have hurt, frustration, some bitterness, and some self-pity. Hopefully, however, they learned something about themselves and about marriage.

Lord, I pray for them. They are both young enough and smart enough to build a home. I like them. They are attractive people. I want them to be happy.

This second marriage route is tough. The road is cluttered with a thousand obstacles and pitfalls. It takes a lot of maturity, a lot of forgiveness, a lot of love to make them work. However that's true of any marriage—first or fifth.

And don't overlook their kids either, Lord. All this is difficult for them. Their former home was unhappy. The divorce was tough. The time they spent without a mom or dad. Now the adjustment to a new parent.

But they need to have two parents and this couple

is determined to make it go. They want to give the children the happiness and security they need and deserve.

Maybe You and I can help.

THE HIT-AND-RUN DRIVER

FATHER, a hit-and-run driver killed a little girl who attended our Sunday school. She was on her way to a store to get a gift. It was her birthday. She was eight years old. She was bright and pretty. Now she is dead. And it was her birthday. Another senseless automobile death.

We've tried hard to help her parents with their broken hearts. They are so confused. So lonely. So sick. It isn't ever easy to be with people in times of death, but the death of a little child is indescribably difficult.

Within a few hours the driver gave himself up. Seems that his conscience was tormented. Couldn't sleep or eat. Couldn't look in the mirror. He was frightened and desperate. I think he has a broken heart too.

So tonight I'm praying for him as well as the parents. His grief is compounded by guilt.

He said he really hadn't been drinking too much. Just enough to dim his vision slightly, just enough to slow his reflexes, just enough to keep him from being able to avoid the child.

And the parents didn't really intend to let the little girl out by herself. They were tired and were watching television, but they weren't really too tired to go with the little girl. So their grief is compounded by guilt.

Our community is very mad at the hit-and-run driver. I'm mad too.

He shouldn't have run away, shouldn't have been drinking and driving. The little girl shouldn't have been on the road. It is all so senseless. And the raving and ranting of citizens is senseless too. Raving won't raise the dead.

But we could all be more careful.

THE KIDS AND DRUGS

FATHER, with all the talk and publicity about drugs, I figured it was just a question of time until it hit my little circle of friends. And that's all it took. Just time.

Both of the girls from our church family have had every apparent advantage. Nice clothes. Their own room. Spending money. Loving parents—at least they act loving. These girls go to good schools and make average grades. They haven't been in trouble at school or with the police.

Over the past month they have been missing school. Found out that they had been sneaking out of their room at nights. In fact, they've done this a dozen times.

The police found them in an apartment last night. Four other girls fourteen and fifteen. Three university students. Boys. The boys rent the apartment. It was all bizarre and kind of unbelievable. Everyone taking pills of one kind or another. Playing records. Eating cold canned soup. Half dressed. Dirty, stinking room. Vomit. Smoking pot. Beer cans.

Now what?

The boys apparently are trying to get the girls hooked. For money? Sex? Are they just mixed up? Are they criminals? Maybe both. Maybe other things add to the complexity of this kind of person. The boys have been arrested, which I think is right. They are dangerous.

The girls are really messed up. Their parents are distressed. Frantic. Panic. Grief. Disbelief. Confusion.

You will have to help me help these kids, Lord. They must get back on the right track before they are completely ruined. And some repair needs to be done before they are ready to proceed.

But it's all pretty rough on everyone concerned.

RIGHT OR WRONG

FATHER, I'm willing to concede that all people have the right to their own religious convictions and practices. That's okay. Some of my own ideas about right and wrong are a little strange to other people.

Some people think it's wrong to cut their hair, others think it's wrong to wear long hair. Some think it's wrong to eat meat, others think it's wrong to eat meat on a certain day. Some think movies, lipstick, short skirts, and tobacco are wrong.

Some people think we should worship on Sunday, some on Saturday, some Friday, and some Wednesday. And in keeping with these ideas people are always anxious to get a law passed to make their special day a legal holy day.

This is the kind of thing I'm thinking about tonight, Father. The tendency people have to try and force, by law, their own peculiar brand of religion on other people. Seems to me that the more difficult it gets for religion, the more apt we are to seek this kind of legal help.

More and more American church people seem to think we can pass enough laws to make people behave properly, make them overcome prejudice, make them care for the poor, make them be kind.

Lord, this really worries me. I'm not so sure I'm right and that all of these other people are wrong. And I certainly don't want the Congress or the Mayor or the taxpayer to do what I'm not able to do, with the help of the Holy Spirit, through the power of persuasion.

This isn't anything new, is it, Lord?

A MAN

FATHER, I was in the coffee shop at the hospital when Dr. Jennings came in. Really don't know him too well. He's a neurosurgeon. Young. Capable. Doubtless he's getting rich. Big house. Big cars. Expensive clothes. A farm. And he has been buying some thoroughbred horses. He has a good reputation with other physicians.

He looked terribly tired. Seems by his conversation that he had been called out pre-dawn to operate on a seventeen-year-old boy who had been broken up in an auto crash.

The boy died.

Dr. Jennings just started talking. This was his third auto accident in four days. Two had died. One was critical. He went on. He had operated on a young father who had a cancerous brain tumor.

He was tired.

Too little sleep. Too much pressure. Too many deaths.

Doctors don't usually pay much attention to preachers. They are busy people. They are used to having people do what they tell them to do, and having them hang on their every word. People have a tendency to idolize the physician's skill and knowledge. They always expect too much of the doctor. And it's easy for doctors to become enamored with their own professional skill.

But You know, Lord, and I think Dr. Jennings knows, that it isn't really that way.

Doctors are, after all, human too. They get hungry, have to cut their nails, catch common colds, need to buy shoes for their kids, learn their spouse's moods, control their dandruff, replace broken shoe laces, and brush their teeth.

And they fail. And they get tired. And patients die.

And for these reasons tonight I'm praying for Dr. Jennings. Another man.

ON WAR AND PEACE

FATHER, there isn't much I can do about war, missiles, bombs, and all that. As long as people are determined to live by force and die in violence the world is likely to stay pretty much as it is.

I think I'm as patriotic as the next guy. We deplore slavery, dictators, Iron Curtains, and the nuclear arms race. No one enjoys freedom more than I do. And we must protect ourselves. I would fight for my family and my country.

The thing that worries me tonight are these two fellows I ate lunch with. Bill and Lewis. Somehow we got off on missiles and war.

They claim to be super-patriots and they're all for bombing Russia, China, or anyone else who disagrees with us. Of course they're mouthing off over a hamburger in an airconditioned restaurant. They don't make foreign policy. Probably have never written to their Congressman and may not even be registered voters. I don't know how sincere they are.

But these guys give me the creeps. Weird. They would sound insane if they didn't sound so calm, so rational. What they say would sound like madness if they didn't say it so logically.

What kind of men talk about destroying millions? Wiping out cities? Risking the destruction of the world?

Well, You know Bill and Lewis. They attend our church. Our luncheon meeting was to discuss ways and means of increasing attendance. They think we ought to be getting more "little children under the influence of the Gospel."

God, I'm sick.

I'M TIRED

FATHER, sometimes I feel as if I'm clinging for my life to an emotional pendulum that keeps picking up speed.

Today I saw Mrs. Anderson who has had a stroke. Talked at length to Joe and Judy who plan to get married next month. Visited Al who is all broken up from an auto accident. Counseled with Ruby whose husband wants a divorce. Stopped in to see the Barkers, old and lonely. Then the Petersons whose only son died in the service. And Fred who is out of work. And George and Marie and their retarded child.

When I meet church members on the street or in the office or in a shopping center they expect me to be friendly, happy, and intensely interested in them. And I am interested. But I'm tired.

Tired of suffering and pain. Tired of sitting helplessly by and listening to dear people tell true stories of hurt and disappointment. Tired of the failures. Tired of things that can't be changed.

But akin to that is my frustration about the things that can be changed. The stupid, dumb things people do. Their ugly self-pity and disgusting self-righteousness. I'm tired of listening to the arrogance and prejudice of too many.

I guess I'm not worth much to You tonight, Father. I'm just fed up. Don't know if anything I did all day has made any difference to anyone. But I did the best I could.

I'm tired. Good night, Father.

THE STREET WHERE I LIVE

FATHER, this morning when I got up a mocking-bird was singing. In the distance I could hear trucks and cars as early risers went to work. The sun was trying to push away the dark, and in that magic moment of dawning I thought about the street where I live.

I visualized it all. The trees, half grown, but growing. Full and green in spring, tall and naked in winter. And I lay in bed for a few minutes and imagined the yards. Flowers. Shrubs. Bicycles. And children. By now I know most of them by name and they know me.

Jack whose daddy deserted him. Five kids in the Boone family who all play in the street. Little Pam who is crippled. Bud and Phil who are becoming teenagers. Sharon who is shy and sometimes just stands at the edge of our porch and looks away in the distance. Paul and his motor bike. The twins next door who have become young women, but I remember them as tomboys, climbing trees. Joan, Sue, and Dave playing "momma and daddy" with my kids and then changing quickly to a game of kick ball. And Carl who rode his bike up and down our street and later died in Viet Nam.

Lord, I pray for the children on the street where I

live. Most of them have a difficult family life; they are helpless and deserve much better.

And all of them have a right to grow up in a peaceful world.

Surely we can do better.

DON'T BE AFRAID

FATHER, the storm was loud. Lightning. Thunder crashing and rumbling. Sheets of rain. Wind crying like a vampire in the night. It woke me up.

My little girl slipped into the bedroom and touched me on the shoulder saying, "It's me, Daddy, don't be afraid." She snuggled into bed with us and soon went to sleep in spite of the storm. Apparently unafraid.

She taught me a lesson, Lord.

So often we come to You with all of our human courage, our insufferable arrogance, our sufficiency. And we try to act big in Your presence. We try to act like You need us.

But we know better, Father. Like my little girl, the sounds of darkness frighten us. The storms are strange and awesome. There are always things we don't understand that perplex us and cause dismay.

For these reasons we have learned to trust You and to call upon You. In the experience of fear and doubt we search for Your hand, listen for Your voice, and try to find security under the blanket of Your love.

When my little girl sought me in the storm, I never

even considered denying her the security of my presence and love.

And You are more than I am. Never again will I wonder where You are in the darkness. I'll listen for You to say, "Don't be afraid."

FOR THE NEW PARENTS

FATHER, this has been a tough day, and tonight I'm thinking especially about Ralph and Betty— new parents today. First child. All the excitement, hope, and anticipation that goes with having a new baby. But the baby has permanent, unchangeable brain damage. He is obviously, finally, and forever mentally impaired.

It's not their fault. Nor the doctors. It has nothing to do with inheritance, or prenatal care, or with delivery. Something was wrong and no one could change it. And no one is blaming You either, Lord. But they probably will in a few days.

They both feel pretty low tonight. The boy will never talk or learn or play like other boys. He will never look or act like other children. He will always need special care. He will never marry, or go to college or become President. He will always be different.

I pray for them. Give them that extra portion of patience they will need. And wisdom. Help them to love him in spite of his abnormalities and in spite of the drastic changes his birth will cause them.

There is so much of life for this little fellow. He

can learn to laugh. To respond to beauty. Music can touch his soul. He can learn simple skills. Best of all he can be loved and can return love. In fact, he will have an extra capacity for love.

Father, I'm sorry he will never be what we consider normal, but You can help us all to be more loving because of him. Grant it, please.

ON ADOPTING A CHILD

FATHER, this young couple, Jane and Wayne, adopted a baby boy today. I'm glad.

Many things today have discouraged me—the cancer patient, the boy in the motorcycle wreck, the kid in juvenile court, the couple with four youngsters trying to get a divorce—but tonight I'm thinking about Jane, Wayne, and the new baby.

True, they didn't give birth to the child. But they are giving him a home. He was conceived by two young people who didn't really want him and who couldn't take care of him. He was conceived by a couple who were unable to provide him a home.

Jane and Wayne wanted a baby. They wanted this little boy. This is no act of passion. No physical accident. He was chosen by them. They picked him out and I like that.

They fixed up his room. They have toys, bed, and all the other things he will need. Most of all, they want him and will love him.

When he is older, he will ask them questions. He won't really understand the word adoption. He will only know that Wayne and Jane have been the only parents he has ever known. They were the first people to love him.

So I pray tonight for Wayne and Jane and their new baby. Bless them. Help them. Guide them. Give that baby good health and give them all happiness.

And, Lord, there are so many other babies in our world tonight who are unwanted, unloved, and uncared for. Find some more Waynes and Janes for these babies too.

HE NEVER WINS

FATHER, I'm concerned tonight about Charley. He's one of those fellows who attends church regularly, always has a friendly smile, and seems happy enough. But I really don't know him too well, and we have never been intimate enough to really be friends.

When he came by this morning to talk to me about his job I was surprised. After ten years at the same industrial plant he has quit his job and invested his savings in a new retailing outfit. It all sounds kind of shaky to me. I never heard of the company and apparently Charley doesn't know much about it either.

I know he is scared to death. But he is trying hard to be optimistic and courageous. Seems that Charley wants to get rich quick and believes he has found the route. Maybe so. Some people do get rich quick in some fields.

He also wants to be independent. Charley says he has never been free. Independent. His own boss. He thinks attorneys, physicians, preachers, and businessmen are independent.

Charley says he never got ahead in his life. Even in Cub Scouts. He was always the tenth man on the baseball team. Always missed the honor roll by a percent. There was always someone else who was promoted ahead of him. He never wins.

Lord, I pray for Charley and for all the people like him in the world who think they never win. Not that You will make them all winners—I don't think winning is very important to You—but that You'll teach Charley how to lose. And help me in this way, too.

MAN ON THE MOON

FATHER, I don't understand the technology and research that made the moon flight possible and successful. It's all beyond me, but I am delighted to have been alive and to have experienced it all.

Now, Lord, the purpose of these trips to the moon as I understand it is to learn something about the moon, the universe, and perhaps about the earth. They want to know how it all began. Where it all came from. And what it's all made of.

That's okay. Many of us believe that You started it all and that the secrets of the universe are in Your hands. But we need to learn all we can.

Frankly, Father, my prayer is that we learn more

about humans than we've known before. People like me aren't too worried about the composition of the moon and other planets. But we are vitally concerned about the composition of people.

Maybe space trips will give us some new inspiration and pride. Seems like we spend a lot of time lately criticizing mankind. Perhaps we'll lift our heads a bit toward heaven.

Maybe this will teach us what we can do when we work together toward the same purpose and under the same discipline. I appreciate the team work involved in space flights

Maybe we will learn the worth of human life. The extraordinary precautions taken to preserve the safety of the astronauts impresses on me the value of human life. And that's right. We might learn to honor life with that same kind of devotion and careful scrutiny. War, starvation, and auto accidents seem so mundane and impossible to believe after space flights. In fact, death by design or by negligence seems vulgar and profane.

Yes, I'm glad to learn something about the moon and outer space, but I pray that we can learn more about people.

THE GUY WITH THREE KIDS

FATHER, I'm praying tonight for my friend Roy, the guy with three kids.

Like most parents, Roy feels inadequate and confused about rearing them. I guess people always wonder if they are disciplining at the right times, if they are setting the right example, if they show enough love, and if they are teaching the right things.

Anyhow, Lord, Roy is upset because his oldest child, a girl, is disinterested in school and too interested in boys. He thinks that the schools are at fault, that she has the wrong friends, and that somehow society has failed. It's probably a little of all these plus the mistakes that he and her mother have made.

But this gets out of perspective to men like Roy.

And he thinks that his two smaller children are heading for trouble. They don't respect him enough, they break things, they don't obey him, and they're lazy. They are boys, six and ten.

Roy and I both agree that he needs to be with the kids more than he is. Go places with them. Take them to church. Talk to them and play with them. And he needs to crack the whip with consistency, rather than blowing his top occasionally.

I wanted to talk to You about it, because You have been watching Your children head for trouble for a long time. I have a feeling that parents like Roy and me worry too much about the wrong things. That we should try it like You do—set up some ground rules, love the kids, and discipline them when they're out of bounds.

And then accept the fact that children inevitably make mistakes.

THINGS LOOK DIFFERENT

FATHER, maybe preachers spend too much time in crises. Births. Sickness. Death. Anyway, we get conditioned to this kind of tension and excitement. We're with people during the most profound moments and we learn to live on that high emotional plateau.

As a result we miss a lot of little things that are important.

This young friend of mine, Bill, is in a coma. I've spent most of this week with his wife and two kids. And You know, Lord, that we've all been praying that he will get well.

This thing about Bill has caused me to slip in this personal prayer.

I have a feeling that I've kind of been in a coma myself. My children talk, laugh, and fuss, and a lot of it goes over my head. The trees in my yard have grown and bloomed, and I didn't sit down to watch them. This morning about 6:00 A.M. the mocking bird sang, and I didn't stop to listen.

Today I picked up an unread book of poetry, played a new song on the piano, and paused to smell a rose.

Bill may never wake up again. And if he does he may not be able to see or hear or smell or speak or even think. But I have the ability to listen to the birds sing, watch the sunrise, smell the honeysuckle, and speak to my loved ones.

Lord, please keep me awake. Deliver me from the coma that attends self-centered activity.

A LOSING BATTLE

FATHER, a couple of people I met today keep popping up in my memory tonight.

There's this woman—past middle age. Way past middle age! She has a fine looking, successful husband, three grown children, and seven half-grown grandchildren. They live in a nice home and she apparently has a comfortable life.

But she is obsessed about her age. She wears too much make-up. She wears too few clothes. It's not that make-up or skimpy clothes really bug me, but in her case it's a rather pitiful effort to appear young and glamorous.

She kept telling me that people never believe she has grandchildren. And that people think she and her daughters are sisters. And that men flirt with her at the club.

This woman is missing so much in life by pretending. I guess she has reasons. But, Lord, she could use some help, and I don't know how to handle that kind.

In contrast I'm praying for the aged widower I visited. He was working with his flowers and plants. Early this morning he had been fishing. When he is tired he takes a nap. He reads. Watches television. Goes to church. Complains when he wants to. Enjoys his grandchildren and gripes about the neighbor's kids.

Nothing phony about this man. He is just what he is.

So I thank You tonight for this man who lives one day at a time without any pretense.

THE CHURCH

FATHER, today has been another one of those days. I keep hassling with people about the make-up of the church. They want to make the church a club with certain kinds of members.

But I've been thinking about our church tonight. What a collection of people! And I'm grateful to You for all of them.

An architect and a couple of truck drivers. The black woman and the hairdresser. A high school football player and a mentally retarded boy. The typical traveling salesman and the lovely young housewife. Electrical engineer and the blind man.

The alcoholic and the little Boy Scout. The retired school teacher and the college student. An unwed mother and the fellow who is the baby's father. The men and women who worry too much, and the ones who never take anything seriously. The woman dying of cancer and the father who races hot rod cars. The nurse. And the politician. The divorced young mother and two couples who celebrated their fifieth wedding anniversary.

Lord, I'm not praying for a perfect church. But I do pray for a church that will help imperfect people. Make the church like a hospital. Send us the sick, the wicked, the troubled. Not that they will all be healed or changed. But send them so we can help them, so they can help us, and so You can help us all.

Just deliver us from prejudging people. Thank You for everything. And especially for the church.

ON BECOMING SIX

FATHER, my little girl is six. That long anticipated birthday finally arrived. She was so excited.

We gave her gifts, her brother gave her the traditional birthday spanking, grandparents came by, her little friends attended the birthday party. It was a big day.

Watching her I tried to remember what it means to be six. At six you run and play until fatigue drives you to bed. You try to count, write, and read. You realize that the school routine will soon begin. Energy. Curiosity. All of these are six.

You don't worry about war and inflation. You assume that all boys and girls are free to run and play. As a middle-class American six-year-old you are not acquainted with terror and oppression. You aren't afraid of police or knocks in the night.

At six you expect to eat. The price or quantity or even the quality of food is unimportant. At six you expect your parents to feed you.

At six you have an amazing ability to trust. To believe. To love and be loved. Your spirit is gay and your hopes are high. You haven't been touched by suspicion and disillusionment. Cynical attitudes aren't born yet.

Birds and flowers. Balls and bikes. Books and music. Bugs and old clothes occupy your time. Your mind isn't cluttered with things like quarrels, prejudice, hatred, and frustration. I remember, Father, that Jesus said that unless we become as children we cannot enter into the Kingdom.

Thank You, Lord, for what it means to be six.

ON APPEARANCE ONLY

FATHER, sometimes I wonder if religion will ever make a lasting impact. Personally I'm not impressed with some of the "new look." But hair length and clothing styles are hardly religious questions. Yet some people persist in discussing them in a religious context.

I remember that Jesus said something about judging things by their outward appearance. He seemed to believe that what was inside the person really made the difference.

Lord, please help us get off this appearance kick. When we try to make fair judgments and be discerning help us to see the person, not his or her clothing or hairstyle.

We are all hung up on how we look. We worry more about how we appear than about who and what we are. Cosmetics, lotions, razors, and shampoos consume a large share of our budgets. Being neat and clean is okay, of course, but we have to keep our focus. And that's not easy.

I guess Jesus had a beard and wore sandals and a long robe. George Washington wore a wig and knee britches. Lincoln had whiskers and a stove pipe hat. But what they wore was not relevant to their greatness.

Lord, You taught us that man looks at the outward appearance but that You look at the heart. Help us to see, as You do, beyond outward appearances.

THE HIGH SCHOOL GRADUATE

FATHER, I've spoken to two high school graduating classes this spring. Like most speakers I've tried to say something to these young people that they will remember, something that will help them. But I know they don't pay much attention to Commencement speakers. So I want to pray for them.

These kids are coming into a confused world. They realize that. Most of the institutions are shaky. The lines are blurred about loyalty and conduct. Family life has changed. They face an unstable society.

To be sure, these young people have more learning than any generation has ever had. Their schools are better than ever before. Their teachers are better trained. Education has given them tools older people never had.

But this hasn't given them security. And it hasn't made the adult world secure about receiving the graduates either.

Lord, I pray that these young people—so strong and handsome, so learned, so talented, so sophisticated—will move into society with compassion.

Yes I pray that You would give them tender hearts. Add the dimension of love and charity to their keen minds and strong bodies. Give them gentle spirits to accommodate their accumulated skills.

Grant them the spirit of loving kindness.

As this graduating class moves into the adult world, may they bring compassion to our distressed society.

THE MOTHER WITHOUT A PARTNER

FATHER, nearly every day some young woman comes by to talk who is divorced and is trying to raise her children without the help of a husband.

Most of them say essentially the same things. They married too young. Or their in-laws messed up the marriage. Or they fussed with their husbands all the time. Or they fell in love with some other man. Or they couldn't agree on money matters. Or the husband drank too much. Or some other reason. Anyway, they took the route of divorce.

After they find out how difficult and painful divorce is, they turn to the church. And again there's trouble. We all know that divorce is tough and church leaders try to prevent it. But sometimes, Lord, we don't reflect much of Your attitude of love and forgiveness. In fact the church can be pretty harsh and inflexible.

Anyway, these people need our help and Yours. They are lonely. They have their hands full earning money, caring for kids, and trying to adjust to the changes.

I pray that You will help them get a new focus on life, help them to overcome their bitterness, give them new friends to ease their loneliness. Give them patience, strength, wisdom, and a sense of humor with their children. Grant them a sense of purpose.

Most of all, Lord, help us to help them. There are a lot of these single parents today. And they can help others.

THE CHILDLESS MOTHER

FATHER, occasionally I've talked with You about some woman who has wanted a baby but couldn't have one. Like Sarah of old, sometimes these women do become mothers, as if by miracle. Others adopt precious children and find joy in their chosen role.

And too often I've talked with You when some mother has given up a child in death. Leukemia. Auto accident. War. This is always tough. Extremely, indescribably painful. Tears and broken hearts. Lord, how we prayed when those children died.

But today I talked with another kind of childless mother. Actually, she gave birth to three children. She carried them in her womb, heard their first cry, held them in her arms, fed them at her breast. They called her mother. But she has had to give up those children. Two are in a children's home, one in a foster home. She rarely if ever sees them. The youngest two have never really known her. They will forget her.

She is poor. She is illiterate. She can't hold a job. She won't pay her bills. She can't drive a car. She wouldn't fix the kids a meal. They were in desperate need, horribly neglected. Finally the social worker prodded her into giving up the children. I don't doubt that the children had to be taken from her even to survive. She just isn't capable of taking care of them in even the most basic way.

Her husband left and apparently disappeared several months ago. There are no other relatives in the city.

Last night she sat alone in her cold, damp, dirty one-room apartment. She is dazed and distressed. She just sits. Unkempt. Desolate. Eating some peanut butter from welfare.

Lord, I pray for this childless mother.

A MAN NAMED CHESTER

FATHER, when the mortician called and asked me to conduct the funeral for the man named Chester, I was perplexed. I didn't know Chester. The mortician said Chester didn't know me either, but Chester's landlady said he listened to me on the radio.

I went out to the cemetery to have a graveside service for Chester. The undertaker gave me a card. Chester was 73. Born in Mississippi. Had two children still in Mississippi. He had died at home. The card had his name, age, and burial place.

The casket was closed so I didn't see Chester's face. There wasn't any family so I didn't find out anything about him. I don't know if he was tall, short. If he liked baseball, or wild flowers, or what made him laugh.

I don't know who Chester loved. Or who he had hurt. I don't know what he did last week. I don't know anything about Chester. Standing there beside that sealed casket, I felt alone, sad, and totally sick.

There were three mourners. The landlady wept a few tears. Another man and woman were coolly indifferent. Chester had no pall-bearers. No flowers. Maybe no friends. No church.

It was so quiet the bird's song was loud and clear in the stillness.

I read a couple of Psalms. Prayed a quiet and rather repetitious prayer. And that was Chester's funeral. The three mourners left quickly.

But now I pray again. Lord, how many lonely, desolate men like Chester live in my city? Help us to find them and to love them. Spare me forever from having to conduct another funeral like Chester's.

THE COLLEGE BOY

FATHER, I've been watching the boy. He's still a boy, although he is old enough to vote, old enough to drive a car, and old enough to get married.

He's not really easy to like, because he isn't really easy to know. But maybe if I knew him better I wouldn't like him even as much as I do now.

His clothes are bizarre. His language is obscene and crude. His hair is combed in the latest weird style. His lips are petulant. He wears a perpetual scowl. His hands move restlessly and he pulls his left ear constantly.

He talks endlessly of sex and drugs. He curses his elders, mocks the church, challenges the police, and commends rock music.

But he is still a boy. And Lord, I think there are some things we can do to help him overcome his past. His parents tried to buy him; they didn't spend much time with him. The church tried to force feed him, and he nearly choked. And too much education nearly overwhelmed him.

He wants attention to be sure, but he also wants to be left alone. He wants to be heard, but he also wants to see some mature leadership. He wants to do "his thing," but he also wants us to do something.

No, I don't really like him much, Father. But he is still growing. Help me to understand him.

THE DOG KILLER

FATHER, he ran over the dog. He was driving down our quiet street too fast to stop. Restless and fast as if he were being chased by chariots of Jehu. So I'm praying again.

He is just a boy, too. Not too long ago he played with dogs himself. He walked with his dog, wrestled with his dog, and fed him.

Then he learned to drive. He traded his dog for a high-powered car. That is part of growing up in our age and it's okay, everyone must grow up. But I wonder how much he has grown.

The little boy and girl who owned the dog heard the dog yelp and scream. The little boy went running from the backyard to pick up the little dead dog. The girl ran into the house calling for her momma.

Later that day they buried the dog in an honored spot in their yard, right next to the dog's house.

And the driver?

Well, Lord, part of that is Your department. I hope the kid in the car will have some pangs of conscience and discomfort. Make him remember the yelping, wounded pup. Teach him something.

If he couldn't avoid the dog, he couldn't have missed a child either. And children on quiet streets do stray away.

And while this is on my mind, Lord, help me to be more careful. Help me to watch for and protect the things children love.

FOR A BOY SCOUT

FATHER, the street was crowded when I saw him. The Boy Scout. Walking erect, measuring his steps, imagining he was on a three-mile hike with the troop. His mind paced off each step as he marched briskly along.

His uniform was clean and pressed. His patches and merit badges adorned his sleeves, breast, and jacket. No General ever wore decorations as proudly.

His eyes were clear and bright. Only eleven-year-old boys have eyes like that. In open wonder they roamed the street. Looking into shop windows, but unimpressed with shoes and suits. Looking at each passer-by, but oblivious to their size, color, or appearance. Wondering eyes covering the street, sidewalk, and shop. Filing away each sight for a later time.

He stopped to watch a policeman write a traffic ticket. And again to look at coins and guns in a pawn shop window. And again to pick up a shining object on the sidewalk.

Untouched at this point by greed, envy, or war. Unmarked by the folly of the adult world. Unspoiled by our stupid sin. Down the street walked the Boy Scout.

Then he bent over on the sidewalk. Soon he was on his knees.

I walked closer where I could see that he was talking to an underfed, sick-looking pup. He picked up the dog and pressed it against his decorated shirt and retraced his steps toward home.

The dog will be all right. So will the Boy Scout.

God, help us to learn when to stop and help.

THE BOY IS DEAD

FATHER, it seems to me I'm going to more funeral homes because of auto wrecks than for old age, heart attacks, or anything else.

I've tried to learn how to comfort people in times of death. Often the family finds some solace in the funeral. By then they have had some time to get used to the idea of death. And when a young person dies of a disease, the relatives kind of accept it as being out of their hands. They feel as if the death was unavoidable.

But this boy who died last night in a high-speed auto wreck doesn't fit into the category. Everyone at the funeral home felt this tragedy could have been avoided. The boy and his friends drive too fast. They are irresponsible and immature. They have been stopped by the police, but nothing happened. They drink and drive and brag about it.

Now the boy is dead.

Lord, this is really a problem. Drunken drivers are killing more and more people on our highways each year. Maybe those of us who are Your children have let this thing slip up on us. We don't say much about safe driving. We don't demand law enforcement on the highways. We don't demand that drunken drivers receive stiff sentences. Preachers never talk about it in the pulpit.

In fact—we are all guilty. And we confess this guilt as being sin.

Someone at the funeral service said that the boy's death was "an act of God." But it wasn't. We can't blame You for our recklessness.

God, help the boy's parents today and help us all to correct an evil.

THE OLD FOLKS

FATHER, I know there is no easy answer. Aging people need the care that new, modern nursing homes can give them. Old age brings so many afflictions of body and spirit that constant supervision and attention is often necessary.

But the homes are so antiseptic. So sterile. So clean. So expensive. The staff is so professional. So precise. So arrogantly sure of themselves. The patients are so unhappy. So dependent. So lonely. So unwanted.

And I'm confused, Lord

In other days the young adults took care of their aging relatives. Not just their parents, but uncles and aunts—even an infirm neighbor. Surely it must have been difficult. The young family had to adjust to the whims, the childishness, and the inconvenience of the aged. But that's just the way it was. Maybe that's just the way it should be now.

I don't know, Lord. All I know is that most of those old people I visited today are pretty miserable. They either complain about the care or complain about being a burden. Some of them are just in a stupor. They're either so sick or so discouraged that they don't even reflect antagonism or self-pity.

And the young adults who place them in the homes aren't happy either. They feel guilty. They wonder what is right.

Somehow we must find a way to help the aged find meaning and happiness in life. Their children need some help too.

We'll have to work on that with Your help, Lord.

ON A HUNGRY CHILD

FATHER, the little girl was playing with my little girl. We noticed that she was hitting the candy dish regularly. When I finally suggested she not eat so much candy, she said she was hungry.

Maybe she is. She could be. Kids do go hungry, I guess. Her folks live in a nice house and they have two cars. They mow their lawn with a power mower. They wear nice clothes, and the little girl wears expensive clothes. They attend church.

Her mother and dad both work. They go out at

night a lot. Is she really hungry? Probably not. At least not for food.

I realize that no one is home to fix her cookies and milk when she comes in from school. Her mother isn't much on cooking, and they visit the drive-in hamburger places regularly. She may be tired of peanut butter and hamburgers.

Lord, this little one is hungry for more than just food, she is hungry for attention. Maybe her parents don't know it. I pray that tonight her mother will fix her supper. That her mother will show her how to dress a doll. I pray that her daddy will hold her in his lap. That he will help her with her school work. That both parents will listen to her stories and answer her questions. I pray that they will kiss her and say a prayer with her. That they will get a fuzzy stuffed kitten for her to sleep with. That they will love her real good.

Father, they didn't get the message. She just told my little girl that the baby sitter is coming tonight. Her dad and mother are going out again. She is still hungry. God bless her.

FOR A MIDDLE-AGED COP

FATHER, I've been thinking tonight about Sgt. Glass. Some things he said this morning stick with me.

He has been a police officer for more than twenty years. It's a real job to him. A career. He has gone to school and has some diplomas and certificates hanging on the wall.

At times he has been in danger. Chasing a wild kid in a high speed race. Arresting an addict. Running down a frightened armed man. But the risk involved in his job doesn't really worry him. In fact, he kind of enjoys that.

He likes to wear a badge and carry a gun. He likes to be a figure of authority and to make people do what he says. And again, most people would.

Sgt. Glass knows that cops make mistakes. There are bad cops, and bad doctors, bad teachers, and bad preachers. You know that too, Lord. Sgt. Glass worries about cops who are cruel, who are stupid, and who err.

But my real concern is his pessimism. He is discouraged and disappointed. He knows the crime rate is rising, more kids are getting into trouble, violence is increasing. He knows people don't respect policemen. They don't respect or fear the law. He thinks it gets worse every day.

Well, Lord, I told him to stick to his job and his commitment. Easy to say to a disillusioned, underpaid, harassed cop. But saying it doesn't change things.

But we need him, Father, and others like him. God bless Sgt. Glass.

SWEETHEARTS

FATHER, I guess I'm just like everyone else: I enjoy watching lovers. Love is a common need of all humanity.

So I thank You for the two teenagers holding hands in the church parking lot. Looking at one another so sincerely. Building plans together that time and other lovers will soon erase. Touched by an unspoiled idealism, they whisper in the first bloom of love.

There are bad kids. And teens are capable of violence, greed, and vulgarity. They can distort and destroy a lot of things.

But these two young lovers, naïve and relatively innocent, made me feel good. They will dream without cynicism. They are not touched today by war or hate. Quite the contrary, their world is small and filled with tenderness and love. Soon enough they will be snatched into reality. So, Lord, give them a few more days of young love.

And I was thinking of the sweethearts I saw at the hospital. The elderly woman said they had been married forty-seven years. She is wrinkled, tired, and old. But the old man is sick. He will probably die. They both know it, but they don't talk to one another about it. They don't have to. After so long in love, you don't have to talk about some things.

Their life together in Kentucky has been tough. There is no idealism left. Too many children, too many debts and disappointments, too many tears. This forty-seven-year love affair has been good and bad.

She sits by the bedside and holds his calloused, but frail hand.

Now Lord, I thank You for sweethearts. For those who know the exciting fragrance of love in first bloom. And for those who grow love until it is strong and enduring like a weathered oak. And I pray for all of us who are in between first flower and full growth.

FOR HARLEM

FATHER, I had to see it for myself. Reading about ghettos and seeing pictures of poverty on TV and in magazines won't do it for me. We all read too much about misery, see too much video pain.

Tonight I pray for Harlem. Garbage on the streets, rats running on the edge of Central Park, dilapidated apartments. Filth. Crowded buildings. Stench. Windows broken and charred buildings that are reminders of the riots. Store front churches. Hand-painted cards advertising funeral homes, dry cleaners, and sex shows. Pawn shops covered with iron bars.

But more than the streets, there were the people. Old men walking with slow steps, women with dull eyes, young men dressed in bizarre costumes, little black kids gathered on corners in animated conversation. Lord, there are too many people packed into that little valley on Manhattan and their life is too hard. It's not right.

When You looked out on a crowded city, You wept. Teach us to look with compassion. Teach us to see the people who are lost in the midst of the buildings, the black top, and the pawn shops.

I'm not sure what the best answer is. But America needs Your help. We need some wisdom and knowledge. We need to know how to house and feed people. We can't keep crowding them into our Harlems.

We need some inner changes. And that's Your department, Lord. Help us to overcome our prejudices that make ghettos, our greed that exploits the poor, and our indifference that ignores them.

I realize I have no right to pray for Harlem and ignore my own people. So forgive me and use me where I am.

ON A BLIND MAN

FATHER, I need to talk to You about Fred Foster, the blind man. It's been too long since I've been by to visit him. No one looks forward to my coming more than he does. I'll try to be more faithful.

What should I tell Him? He has this idea that someday he will get some new eyes from the eye bank and some marvelous surgeon in New York or Houston will be able to plant new eyes in his head. Every doctor tells him it can't be done. But he doesn't listen to them. To them he is as deaf as he is blind.

Not that he is miserable or useless. He does a good job with his telephone answering service. Enjoys listening to the radio and reads Braille very well. He likes clothes and always looks neat and clean. He's lonely, of course. But I know a lot of sighted people who are lonely.

It's not really his blindness that concerns me. On a day-by-day basis he seems adjusted. He earns enough to stay comfortable. And he does have some friends. Not many. But some. He can't see children or flowers or television or a sunset—and that's nearly inconceivable to me. He's been blind since he was four.

But what about this eye transplant business, Lord?

We always get to that. He is just kidding himself. There is nothing there. Science says it is impossible. And they tell him so. Time and again they tell him so. Today I tried to tell him too. He keeps talking about the future that can't happen. How can we make him stop dreaming of miracles in the future?

Miracles in the future, Lord? Or what is heaven for?

ON LOSING A FRIEND

FATHER, Joe is sore at me. I guess this thing between us has been brewing for months. At least our friendship has been tense lately. He probably feels I've been treating him differently, and I know he has been more restrained toward me.

It's strange. For the last couple of years we have been good friends. Fishing together. Ball games. Drinking coffee. He has told me more about his real estate business than I really needed to know. But that was his idea, not mine. He always supported me in the church program and acted like he agreed with my sermons.

You know what tears Joe up, Lord. It's the race question. As nice and congenial as he is, he really has this thing about blacks. Funny how excited and nearly irrational he can get when the subject comes up. Nothing moderate about Joe.

I know the open housing legislation affects realtors emotionally! But I'm not sure that open housing laws really make much difference one way or the other. It won't actually affect Joe's income or his rights. That's what I tried to say to him.

But he sure exploded. Went through all of that speech about keeping politics and socialism out of the pulpit. That preachers who live in church-owned houses ought to keep quiet about open housing. And besides, he says, church property should be taxed. He's mad all right.

I'm uneasy, Father. Probably I've been unfair to Joe these past two years. We simply haven't discussed the race question because I didn't want to offend him. I know there is no real value in being deliberately offensive, but my obvious reluctance to introduce the subject must have made him think I agreed with him.

Evidently I've lost a friend. And I don't have enough to spare one. Maybe my silence for two years was too costly.

A BROKEN BIRD EGG

FATHER, may I make this confession? This morning when my little girl came in I was busy at the desk. Usually she doesn't interrupt my work and always seems to be glad when I'm working at home.

Anyway, she was all excited about a broken bird egg in the back yard. She was worried about the mother bird. About the little unborn bird. And mostly about the broken beauty of the egg. She wanted me to go look. But I didn't have time to look at a broken bird egg.

You know how it is, Father. Preachers stay busy trying to mend up things. People have broken hearts because of death and disease. The world seems to be breaking up over war and hatred. Homes break up when husbands and wives let their vows fall into disrespect. It's not that broken things are strange to preachers. Quite the contrary! We spend most of our time trying to put pieces back together.

But this has worried me all day. Sure, she left my study quietly. She didn't cry or even protest my indifference. We didn't have a scene about it. After all, it was just a broken bird egg.

My little girl cared, though, Lord. That's what stuck with me until now. This was a crisis, a sadness to her. And her dad ignored her hurt and concern. I was wrong. God grant that she will always be hurt by the broken things. That she will always care.

As for me being too busy to pause for a broken bird egg, I remember now about One who watches even a sparrow. Next time, if there is another time, I'll be more concerned, Lord.

ON SUNDAY NIGHT

FATHER, I'm always tired on Sunday night. It's not so much the preparation and delivery of sermons. Nor the incessant demands of the rushing people in the church organization. Nor the awesome business of trying to talk about You to the congregation, although I still don't have either the knowledge or the nerve to tell them what I really think about You.

Mrs. Williamson is the one who bugs me tonight. She keeps me off balance, Lord. Living in that house trailer. Alone. Half blind. Hoping against hope her son will get out of prison before she dies. And what if he does? He will just break her heart again. He's a worthless wretch who will never reform. So if her prayers are answered and he does get home, she will tell me how great it is. And if she dies first—well, she will die believing her boy will reform. Maybe that is hope.

It's funny about hope, Father. That's why I'm weary on Sunday night. I don't have as much as Mrs. Williamson. Sure I preach about it, but then I take everything too seriously. Hope doesn't grow where there is so much self-importance. Or self-confidence. We have to depend on You. That's not faith as much as it is hope. Hope that You can deliver us out of the intolerable mess we make of things as we plot and plan with so much self-confidence. Then it goes awry. And we try to blame someone else for our stupid mistakes. This is a special problem for preachers, at least for this one.

That's it. I'm not so tired from the business of running the church today. I'm tired of myself. Especially that part of myself that is so self-sufficient and cocky. Mrs. Williamson has condemned me today. There is someone like her every Sunday. Plain folks. With tremendous problems. Yet there she sits in church listening attentively to me, singing songs to You. She sort of irritates me. I envy her and dislike her for her hope. What can a fellow like me do for her.

I'm tired, Father. Bless Mrs. Williamson and give me some of her hope.

FOR A POOR MAN

FATHER, there really was no easier way to do it. I know the fellow was embarrassed and probably resentful, although he didn't show it too much. There wasn't anything in the house except an old couch with springs broken through and that dirty hot plate. Not a curtain at the window, not a rug, not a chair, not a bed.

The kids are three, four, and six. Eating brown beans and corn bread in a bowl. He said he could buy the food if I could help him find some furniture. He has found a job. He was holding the little boy in his arms as I hold my little boy.

Somehow the war against poverty has missed him. He says he tried four different government and community agencies. Maybe I am too suspicious, Lord, but I called up to check his story. He had told me the truth.

So we got him some furniture. The people brought in enough furniture to take care of five families. He acted grateful, but I know he was embarrassed. I was too.

But what now, Lord? How can we help the guy gain some self-respect? How can we get him out of that dilapidated shack? How can we get him started on a better road? He is working and earns enough that charity shouldn't be perpetually necessary. But he needs more than a new bed or a new house or more money.

He needs a friend. Someone to really care. I understand that because I need friends too. Maybe that's it. He and I both need a friend. We will help and support one another.

I'll try to work on this one, Father.

BIRTHDAY

FATHER, today is my birthday. Time doesn't mean much to You, but it is important to those of us down here. Even those of us who believe in eternal life cling to each day we have here.

Not that I feel old or tired or useless. But another year has past. And this means a lot of opportunities are gone too. Gone forever.

But on my birthday I'm thinking more positively. Not about getting older or about things still undone. I'm remembering the people of the past, Lord.

My mother and dad. They are older now, but they've been around for all of my birthdays. My own kids get a big kick out of me blowing out candles at my age, but they will never know what a kick I get out of everything they do. They have been good gifts, Father. Thanks.

It's taken these passing years to build a good home. My wife and I need these birthdays. By now our home is built pretty solid. We do love one another. And thanks for that, too.

This birthday recalls friends of yesterday and today. It has taken some years to solidify some older relationships and to find people for new and exciting friendships.

Happy Birthday? It sure is. Just to be with people I love is enough this year. And it has taken every year of my life to get here. Thank You, Father, for the gift of life.

THE LITTLE WOOD CARVER

FATHER, the little boy was sitting on the porch step when I drove by. I drive by his house nearly every day on my way to the hospital, so I see him often. His family attends our church.

Today he was carving. For some reason I stopped. Guess You know the reason.

Don't see people carving much any more. I remember some old men in my hometown who sat around and whittled. They sat in front of stores or on benches by the courthouse. One old fellow made me a whistle once. As a boy I tried to make some things with wood and knife. Without much success.

With a dull old pocketknife the little boy was trying to carve a dog's head out of a piece of hardwood. Didn't look much like a dog's head. He knew that. In fact, he said it didn't look like anything. But he kept on carving.

Told me that his dad had taught him to carve.

His dad doesn't live there anymore. He decided a couple of years ago to leave the little boy and the little boy's mother. His dad married another woman. That didn't work out too well and the dad is looking again.

I went through the entire mess with them. The little boy's mother was pretty hard to get along with. Complained all the time. Nagged. Found fault. Was lazy. Of course, the dad was wrong too. A playboy. Irresponsible. Childish. So they broke up.

Now the little boy tries to carve a dog's head with a dull knife and a hard piece of wood.

Guess that's about all his dad tried to teach him.

ABOUT LOSING

FATHER, whenever we're involved in any kind of contest, we always say "someone has to lose." Basketball. Amateur show. Political campaign. Prize fight.

Any time we try to match skills or enter competition or put ourselves on the line against someone else, we calculate the chances of winning or losing. It is so easy to figure out the winner in a ball game or a political campaign. Just count the score or the votes and you have a winner. And a loser.

But it isn't simple in life. There really isn't any way to count, measure, or weigh out the stuff of winning and losing. No computers have been invented that give us those kinds of answers.

Most of us have some goals. They may be clear. Or vague. There are some ways that we determine success. And happiness. And usefulness. Sometimes we stop and consider our accomplishments in our goal-seeking.

And we know when we're losing. When we have been side-tracked. When we have lost our purpose. When our goals have been obscured. We know sorrow. Pain. Defeat. We lose.

Lord, what about losing? How can we learn to accept life's disappointments with more grace? How can we learn to keep going when we're actually losing ground? So many things happen to us that we aren't prepared for. Things we don't expect. Things beyond our control. We get misplaced. With no real options.

I guess we need to remember: You don't keep

score like we do. Your vision is better than ours for You see yesterdays we've forgotten and tomorrows we can never believe.

Maybe we don't lose so often after all.

AN INTERRUPTION

FATHER, in common with most people who try to keep some kind of schedule, I don't like interruptions. Every night before I go to bed I look over my calendar for the next day. Things to do. Meetings. Visits. And normally I achieve most of those goals during the day. That's the only way I can operate with any peace of mind or efficiency.

But then there are interruptions.

Not that I keep such a rigid schedule. I expect things to change. Pastors, like everyone else, soon learn that outside forces often dictate the use of time. They must be flexible.

The interruption in my schedule this week has been the alcoholic. And I'm being polite, Lord. He is really an old-fashioned drunk. Profane. Obscene. He is dirty with his own vomit. Kicking over furniture. Wants to argue.

He was at the office this morning when I got there. He was on the phone twice during the night. He slept in my car another night. He has been turning up and calling two or three times a day for a week.

I'm so tired. Tired of his noise. Tired of his interference, his interruptions.

But I realized tonight when I started to pray this

prayer that I haven't really been listening to him. Or trying to help him. He has just been an interruption.

Forgive me for such arrogance.

Makes me wonder? Do I interrupt any of Your heavenly schedules when I call? Or do You keep schedules?

A QUIET TIME

FATHER, it was too chilly to sit on the porch. Crisp March night. But there were too many noises inside. Sound and clamor all day. The house is full of sound. The furnace hums. Electric lights buzz. Refrigerator noise. Dripping faucet. Creaking floor.

So I went outside.

There were still sounds, city sounds. A screaming siren. Screeching tires. Rumbling trucks. A jet plane far out of sight. And some country sounds not quite drowned out by those from the city. A night bird singing to its mate. A chorus of crickets without one discord. A big gray cat quietly crossing the yard.

Funny how you can erase the noise of trucks, planes, and sirens. They still scrape against the silence, but you don't hear them. I slowly shut the door on everything but the bird and the whisper of the soft March wind. And in time I shut that out too.

Half awake. Half asleep. Half here and half there. Not listening to anything and yet intently listening for something so still it can't be heard. Deaf to noise, but finely tuned for mystery.

And I don't see either. How long ago did the cat

cross the yard? When did that star come out? The moon moved, but I wasn't watching. A car moved up the street, but I missed that too.

Hearing and sight and time have slipped by.

Half way here and half way there.. Half awake and half asleep. A few, or was it many, magic moments. Didn't worry. Didn't plan. Didn't talk. Didn't listen. Didn't see. Didn't count.

A chilly March night on the porch. Thanks, Lord.

A TRIBAL GOD

FATHER, in common with most religious workers I'm constantly studying my own personal ministry to find evidences of Your presence and approval. And most of my praying is for Your help in those areas where I live and work.

And when things seem to be going good in my own church, I'm very confident that You are indeed a loving and active God. However, when things aren't going well in my territory I have some doubts about Your ability to help. I don't admit this to You very often, but it is true. If my efforts are sluggish and unproductive I begin to wonder where You are. And what You're doing? Wonder if You're doing anything at all.

I guess at that point I fall into a kind of paganism. You become my own private Deity. A tribal God. It is kind of like having my own totem pole. Or personal medicine man. Or household idol.

Usually at those times of building totem poles,

something happens to remind me that You are busy in other places too. With other people. Doing things that need to be done. Not always according to my plans. Or doing things I think You should do.

Missionaries in foreign lands. A Billy Graham Crusade in Australia. A store front group in Brazil. All of these things help me see You. See what You're doing.

I know You don't run Your train on my track. I'm glad for that. Help me get my car hooked up to Your train.

A GOOD NIGHT KISS

FATHER, in former times people developed family traditions and customs, but we have lost that kind of thing today. People move more often. Parents and kids are home less. We usually don't live close to our relatives. We have less time or less inclination to develop family customs.

I've been thinking about this lately, Lord.

What kind of stories will my children have to tell their children about our home life?

They may remember certain things about vacations. And about breakfast. Church attendance. Saturday mornings. Christmas celebrations. Thanksgiving dinners. They probably will remember things we have forgotten. Or things we thought unimportant at the time. They will recall some hurts and disappointments. They will remember some important pleasures that were simple.

There really isn't any way we can program a system of memory for our children. They are not necessarily impressed with the events that impress us. I guess we will always have a problem about this.

Anyhow, Father, I believe that the most consistent custom at our house, and perhaps our most memorable tradition, is the good night kiss. It's important to me. And to the children. Even when I'm out late, they expect me to come to their room and kiss them in their sleep. And I always do.

I'm not sure how long they will remember these good night kisses. But I'll always remember.

So it's worth something to me.

And I need a memory too.

LONELY

FATHER, the man says he was born in North Carolina about forty years ago. He is a chemist and works in the labs at one of the big plants here in town. He is short, too fat, and has bad eyes.

Seems that he married while he was in college and his wife died during childbirth. He loved her. The baby lived. A son. He tried to raise the boy, but gave up and put him in a home when the child was three. The boy was adopted when he was four.

For various reasons he never remarried. Lived in Florida, California, New York, and Iowa. He came to Kentucky six years ago.

He doesn't think much of his parents. Says they were never close. He went back to North Carolina for his mother's funeral. Only stayed there the day of the funeral. He has an only sister whom he doesn't like. She doesn't like him. His father lives with this sister.

He sends them a Christmas card. They don't send him Christmas cards.

He is an alcoholic. He measures his drinks like he measures chemicals in the lab. He never gets too drunk to walk or to talk or to work. He lives in a nice apartment. The walls are lined with books he doesn't read. A color TV he doesn't watch. He plays a stereo constantly. He drinks measured amounts from the time he gets home from work until 9:00 P.M. Sleeps. Gets up. Drinks measured amounts until time to work.

This morning he called, said he was going to kill himself. I didn't know him. Have spent four hours with him and still don't know him.

Lord, help him. Help me help him. He is sick. Confused. Desperate. And lonely.

MELVIN, THE BLACK CHILD

FATHER, I'm white. That's not anything to brag about or to apologize for. My parents and grandparents are white. The color of my skin is an accident of birth. It has nothing to do with my will, my choice, or my worth.

Melvin is black. And that's not anything for him to brag about or to apologize for. His parents are black. His color is not his choice and it does not affect his worth.

Melvin is one of more than one hundred black people who attend our church. Black people in predominantly white churches are exceptions. Rare. Unusual. They are conspicuous in a sea of one thousand white faces.

I'm forty years old. Melvin is thirteen. I am pastor of that church. Melvin attends regularly.

He is a roughneck. He talks too much. Curses the teachers. Fights. Pushes. Won't stay in class. He keeps things in an uproar. He is a badly behaved child. He needs desperately to be disciplined. And like all children, he needs to be loved.

It's not hard to discipline Melvin. He gets into so much trouble. There is always a reason to correct him, to punish him. He expects it. He needs it.

And it's not hard to love him. He has a delightful curiosity. The quickest smile. The most receptive face. At times he is an attractive, nearly charming boy.

His black skin complicates it. If we correct him or fuss at him or punish him, he accuses us of picking on him because he is black. He learned this early in life and uses it consistently to put off discipline.

If we love him overly, he accuses us of being patronizing and of using him because he is black. He is skeptical of us at best.

This isn't easy, Lord. It is tough. At times it seems easiest to let Melvin go away and stay away. But that isn't right either. You will have to help us. And Melvin.

FOR BILLY GRAHAM

FATHER, a strange unprecedented thing happened in our city recently. Some of Billy Graham's people called and said that Mr. Graham could come here for a crusade.

The entire city became excited. Front page in the newspaper. Stories on radio and television. People talking about it on the streets. Truck drivers, farmers, shoe salesmen, ministers, insurance agents, Judges, physicians, plumbers, housewives, nurses, school kids. It became the topic of conversation.

Billy Graham.

According to the Gallup Poll, he is the most admired man in America today. Marshall of the Rose Bowl Parade. Confidant of four U. S. presidents. He has preached to more people than any man in the history of the church.

Billy Graham.

A North Carolina farm boy. No formal theological training. No fancy seminary degrees. Doesn't pop off. Or hire press agents. Stays out of trouble. Married to his first wife. Father of five children. Preaches about Jesus, sin, the Bible, and conversion.

Billy Graham.

People crowd stadiums to hear him. Night after night they come. 58,000. 65,000. 102,000. It's hard to believe unless you are there to see it.

Somehow this preacher represents a miracle in our time. And I pray for him. And for us. We need someone to admire. We need a man we can respect.

Sure, Lord, we need You and Your love and care. But we also need a man, a man like other men, whom we can admire.

Take care of Billy Graham. We all need him.

THE GOLDEN RULE

FATHER, this old man asked me a question today. He asked me, "Whatever happened to the Golden Rule?" He said when he was a boy people talked about loving your neighbor as you loved yourself. They said that you should treat people as you wanted to be treated.

Lord, I don't really know what happened to the Golden Rule. Somehow the church got hung up on other things. We argue about baptism, speaking in tongues, tithing, birth control, celibacy, communism, and a lot of other things. We keep trying to get people to believe a certain way. And if a group cannot agree with some other group on a certain belief, we make a new church. In fact we tell them that what they believe is more important than what they do, that doctrine is more important than love. We forget conduct, compassion, and commitment. We build our churches.

Maybe we threw out the Golden Rule because it was too tough. It is easier to agree on the length of hair, baptism by immersion, or the confessional than it is to be agreeable with our neighbor.

It's hard to love our neighbors when we ourselves don't have much self-respect. This is part of the problem too. When we don't like what we are, we don't really like other people.

Well, Father, I've decided I can't improve on what

Jesus said. My children need to learn the Golden Rule. And the people in our church need to learn the Golden Rule. And the people in our church need to practice the Golden Rule. And so do my neighbors.

So do I. Help me, Lord.

MR. PRESIDENT

FATHER, the other day I went to a prayer breakfast in Washington. The president of the United States was there. And so were a lot of cabinet members. And Supreme Court justices. And congressmen. And ambassadors. And ordinary people like me.

When the president came in all the people stood. He was accompanied by his wife. An entourage of aides. Alert young security men. Billy Graham.

The president walked quickly to his seat. Acknowledged the standing crowd. Sat down. He drank orange juice. Ate sausage. Drank coffee.

I guess he is the most powerful man in the world. At least one of the two or three most powerful. It's hard for me to imagine the importance of his job to so many millions. It's hard for me to understand the trappings of his power. His influence. The details of that kind of influence.

So I watched him sip his coffee.

Billy Graham prayed. I was impressed with his prayer. Prayed for the poor. For peace. For Mr. President. And for our enemies.

The chief justice prayed too. And he made a

speech about prayer. If he doesn't ordinarily pray, he at least knows what prayer is and who ought to pray.

Then the president spoke. He said we needed Your help. Said that he knew that no man, including himself, could do the right thing without You. Said that we all needed an understanding heart and that understanding was a gift from You.

And I felt differently. The president was admitting weakness. Confessing weakness. Acknowledging he needs Your help. Sounded like my own prayers.

So, tonight I pray for Mr. President. He asked me to pray for him.

A LITTLE BOY

FATHER, a certain little boy came to Sunday school last week. No socks. No underwear. A dirty summer shirt. A jacket at least three sizes too big. He has blue eyes, blond hair. He is four years old.

He had been beaten.

Ugly, swollen marks on his little back. They were too sore to touch. They showed through his torn summer shirt. They were crimson red and blue and purple and orange and green. The welts and marks were old and new. Some were fresh and some were healing. He had been beaten before.

He has a broken finger. In fear he had raised his hand to protect himself from the blows. His little hand is swollen to twice its normal size.

His eyes are empty and hollow. Fear and terror mark them with shadow. Glazed. But little yellow lights, like pins and needles, pierced me from back in the shadows. Stranger eyes. They still haunt me tonight.

He can't talk very well. A speech impediment born in ugly fear. When he does talk it is disorganized and incoherent. But he cries a lot. Sobs that come from down deep in his empty little belly. Sobs that come from his broken, lonely heart. Sobs that root deep in his limited little brain. Sobs that cry from his miserable soul.

He begged the Sunday school teacher to keep him. She rocked him in a chair. Spoke sweet words of love. And she was nearly incoherent too. Speechless with frustration. Mute with shock. Wanting to change this tragedy.

He went to sleep.

We contacted the officials. Maybe they can help. But we can help. Oh Lord, please help that little fellow tonight. Please.

GEORGE

FATHER, he was unshaven. Not a modern, neatly trimmed beard. But a long, dirty, uneven beard. His name was George.

He was dirty. Rolls of soot and accumulated dust in the creases of his forehead and cheeks. Dirt in his ears. Grimy, black hands. Broken, filthy fingernails. One thumb was missing.

He smelled like dirt. Grease. That peculiar and unmistakable smell of poverty. The stench of old clothes. Of an unwashed body. His hair was long and stinking. Coarse and brittle hair. I wonder if his hair had ever been washed. Ragged clothes.

He was crippled. Had a peg leg. Not a manufactured artificial limb. A peg leg. Hand carved. It too was dark and greasy. The stump of his knee set loosely in a patched leather apparatus on top of the peg leg.

He said that he had lost the leg in Virginia. Riding a freight train. Railroad detective shot at him. He rolled off the train and his leg was mangled. The leg was still sore. It also had an odor. Unpleasant, ugly.

He had been to Cincinnati, Dayton, and Detroit. Said he was looking for work. People wouldn't hire him because he was crippled.

He was standing in a filling station. Pouring rain outside. Nearly midnight. The station closed at midnight. He wanted to go to West Virginia.

No money.

Yes, he was hungry. Yes, he needed bus fare. Yes, he would appreciate a ride to the bus station.

So I gave him money to buy food, bought a bus ticket. Put him on a bus. Watched him ride off.

It wasn't a cup of cold water. Instead, hot coffee, roast beef sandwich, and bus ticket to Beckley, West Virginia. And a prayer.

ON SAYING NO

FATHER, a woman was in my office today with her little boy who is five. I believe he was the worst kid I've ever seen. Impudent. Impulsive. Absolutely incorrigible. Rude. He climbed over furniture. Knocked everything off my desk. Ran in and out of the building. Out in the street. Screamed. Cried. And she was as impassive as the sphinx.

I finally suggested to her that she had better take this boy in hand or she was going to have a real problem. She already has a problem.

She told me, "I just can't say no to him."

Seems to me that this mother is missing something. Missing something about love. Children of all ages expect their parents to say no. They want their parents to say no. Saying no gives the child the security of parental care and parental discipline. No is often the expected answer. Kids need our help and support in establishing boundaries for conduct and living.

One of the most loving and helpful things my mother and dad ever did for me was to say no. And I remember some times that I even wanted them to say no.

Not that this is all a new idea. Those of us who are Your children have learned that You say no too. We ask and receive not. We look and don't find. We knock and the door is closed. At these times we realize that you're saying no because You know what is best. And You love us enough to say no.

Thank You for not making the same kind of "Yes" mistakes that we make.

FOR OTHER PREACHERS

FATHER, I often think that the best proof of Your love is the tolerance that You show toward preachers. Especially this preacher. Seems that from the very beginning You have chosen an unlikely group of people to build a church. It all started with tax collectors, fishermen, and other common men. And throughout the history of the church You have used a chosen group with limited credentials.

Most of these fellows enter the professional ministry with hesitation and misgivings. They don't expect wealth. Or fame. Or influence. If they expect an easy life, they learn better very soon. Most of them enter the ministry a little scared, and the best ones are still scared the day they die.

People try to impose certain morals and manners on the preacher. People decide how he should speak, behave, and dress. People create images of the ministry. Often they put him up on a pedestal. Maybe the preacher is even dumb enough to encourage them to build it for him. Then he falls from that lofty perch.

I pray tonight for the foolish people who try to make preachers more than they are. And I pray for those of us who are foolish enough to believe it ourselves.

Probably we worry more about our weaknesses than most people do. Any kind of self-examination is always embarrassing. Seeing ourselves as we are. Seeing what people expect. And knowing what we really are. It is at this precise point that we need your help.

And we need one another. So I pray for preachers.

TALKING TOO MUCH

FATHER, I was a guest at a party the other night. It was a rather large group of people. Everyone was laughing and talking. Having a good time. They had a lot in common. They enjoy one another. They're good people. No one in that group would consciously hurt anyone. They were all Christians.

Somehow the conversation and humor turned to an old story about a black man. This led to another. And another. Eventually four or five people were telling jokes about blacks.

Then a black man came in to announce dinner.

Most of us were surprised that he was there. We didn't know the host and hostess had a man helping fix the meal. Some of us were embarrassed. Some of us were humiliated. We shouldn't have talked so much.

The black man ignored our ignorance.

I don't know what he really thought. He was preparing the meal because he is a cook, not because he is black. It was a job. And an honorable job. That's not what bothers me. What concerns me is that we were all doing a lot of talking and became unaware of who we were or where we were. There was a selfish insensitivity in the entire experience. This is the kind of thing we do over and over again.

We say things about people that we just would not say to them. Some of this is understandable. Probably necessary and certainly normal. But we do it too often. You know that and I know that. Forgive us and help us to bridle our tongues.

A SMALL PLEASURE

FATHER, maybe this isn't important to You. But, I believe that You're always interested in those things that give Your children small pleasures.

Today I stopped the car and watched some boys playing baseball. They had their caps, gloves, and bats. Funny. A couple of boys can start tossing a baseball and the sound of ball hitting glove will attract other boys from six blocks away.

And the boys will hit the ball. Or pitch. Not many want to chase fly balls. Or be the catcher. And balls always get lost in the woods.

There isn't anything much more exciting than a home run. Or a double with the bases full. Or striking out the last batter in the last inning.

And can anyone feel more dismal that the boy who strikes out with the winning run on third? No one except perhaps the shortstop who makes a bad throw and lets in the winning run?

Just sitting there watching those boys play ball took me back to my own baseball days. I guess that it's easier to relive that part of the past than anything else. I can remember the black bat I carried around. And my old glove. Worn out spikes. A hot July 4th double-header at Belleview. Walks. Doubles. Strike-outs. New uniforms. Umpires.

And I'm grateful for one of life's small pleasures. Something that is pleasantly and agreeably distracting.

It's back to the world of tension, sin, failure. Death. Pain. Church building. Divorce. Cancer. Auto wrecks. Alcoholism. Broken hearts.

As I drove away a boy was chanting, "Come on, Joe, put it right by him." The kid lined a clean hit over third and a run scored. And I'm glad the run scored.